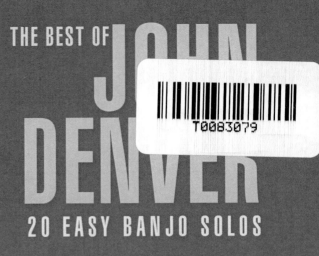

THE BEST OF JOHN DENVER

20 EASY BANJO SOLOS

Banjo arrangements by Harold Streeter

Photo: Pictorial Press Ltd / Alamy

Cherry Lane Music Company
Director of Publications/Project Editor: Mark Phillips

ISBN: 978-1-60378-960-8

Visit our website at www.cherrylaneprint.com

ANNIE'S SONG

Words and Music by
John Denver

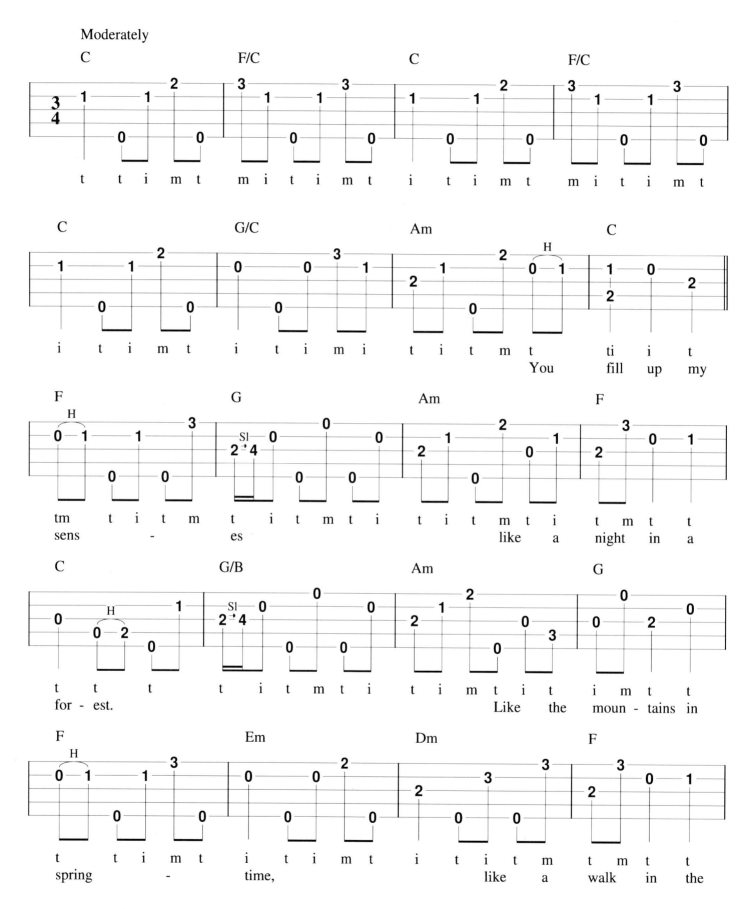

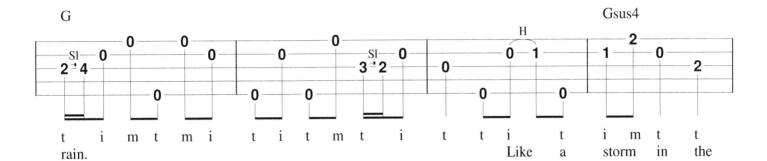

t i m t m i t i t m t i t t i t i m t t

rain. Like a storm in the

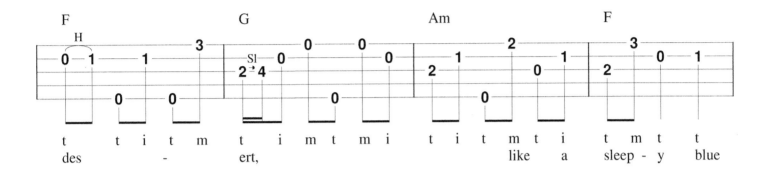

t t i t m t i m t m i t i t m t i t m t t

des - ert, like a sleep - y blue

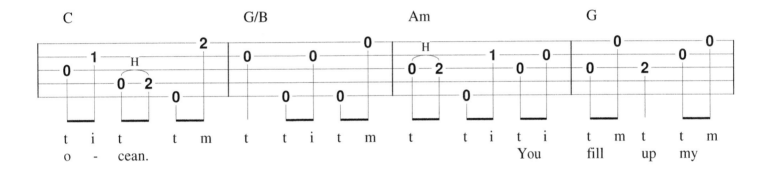

t i t t m t i t m t i t i t m t t m

o - cean. You fill up my

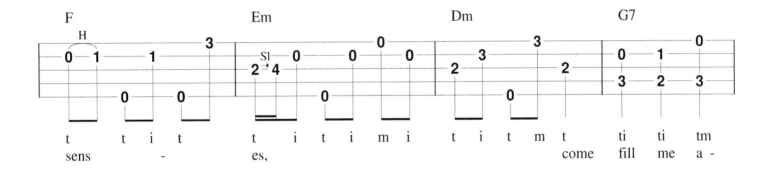

t t i t t i t i m i t i t m t ti ti tm

sens - es, come fill me a -

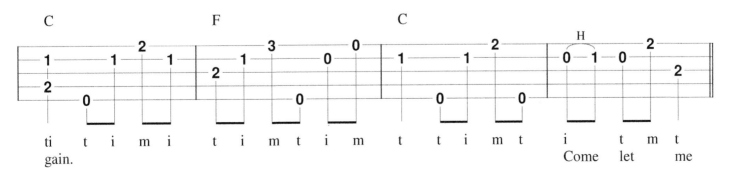

ti t i m i t i m t i m t i t m t i t m t

gain. Come let me

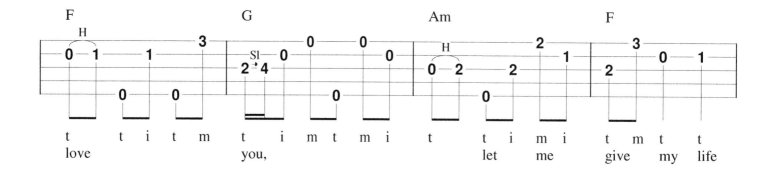

t t i t m
love

t i m t m i
you,

t t i m i
let me give my life

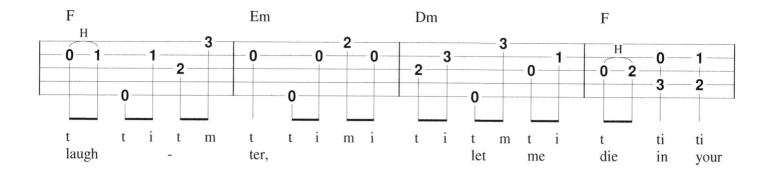

t i t t i
to you,

t i m t m i
let me drown in your

t t m i t i m t t
laugh - ter,

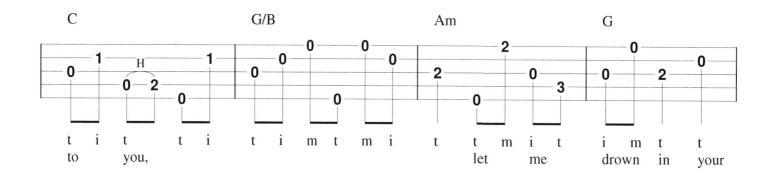

t t i t m
laugh - ter,

t t i m i
let me die in your

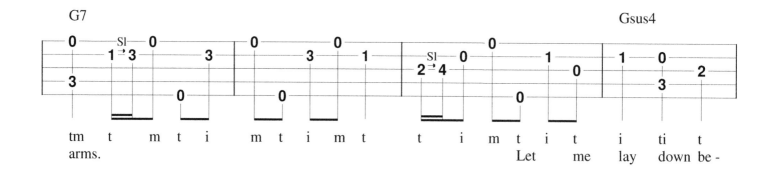

tm t m t i
arms.

m t i m t
let me lay down be -

i ti t

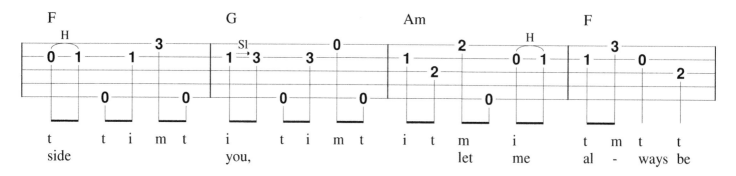

t t i m t
side

i t i m t
you,

i t m i
let me al - ways be

t m t t
ways be

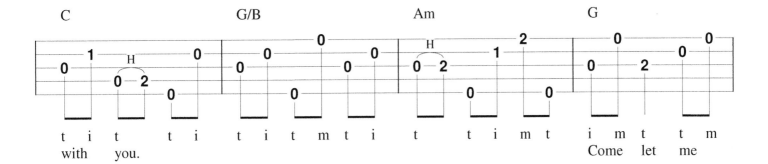

t t i   t i   t i t m t i   t   t i m t   i m t   t m
with you.   Come let me

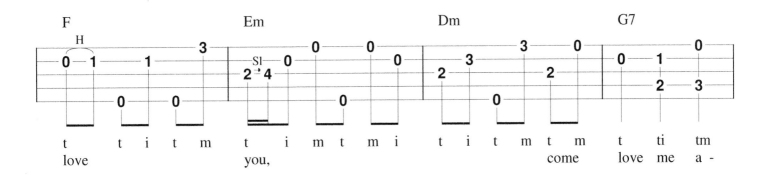

t   t i t m   t   i m t m i   t i t m t m   t   ti   tm
love   you,   come   love me a -

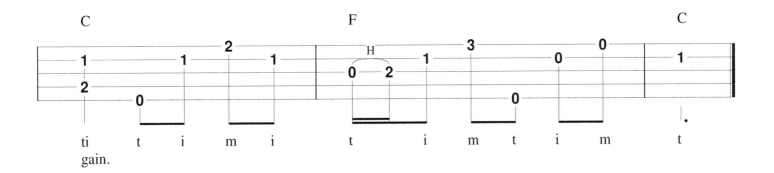

ti   t i   m   i   t   i   m t   i   m   t
gain.

BACK HOME AGAIN

Words and Music by
John Denver

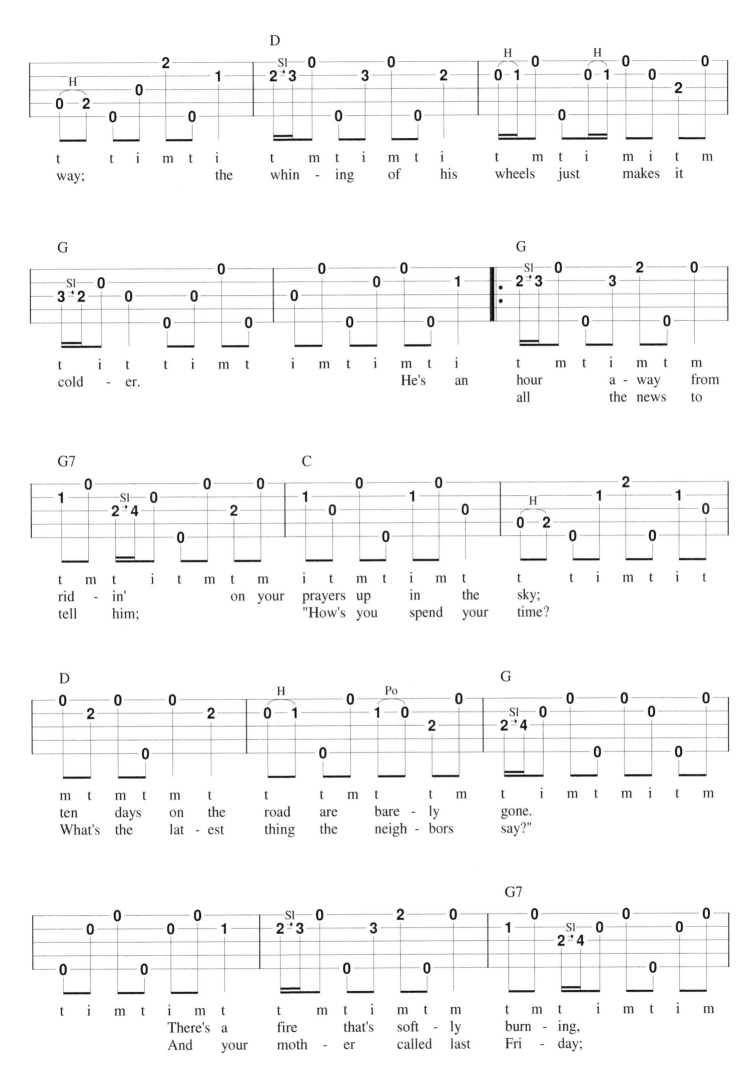

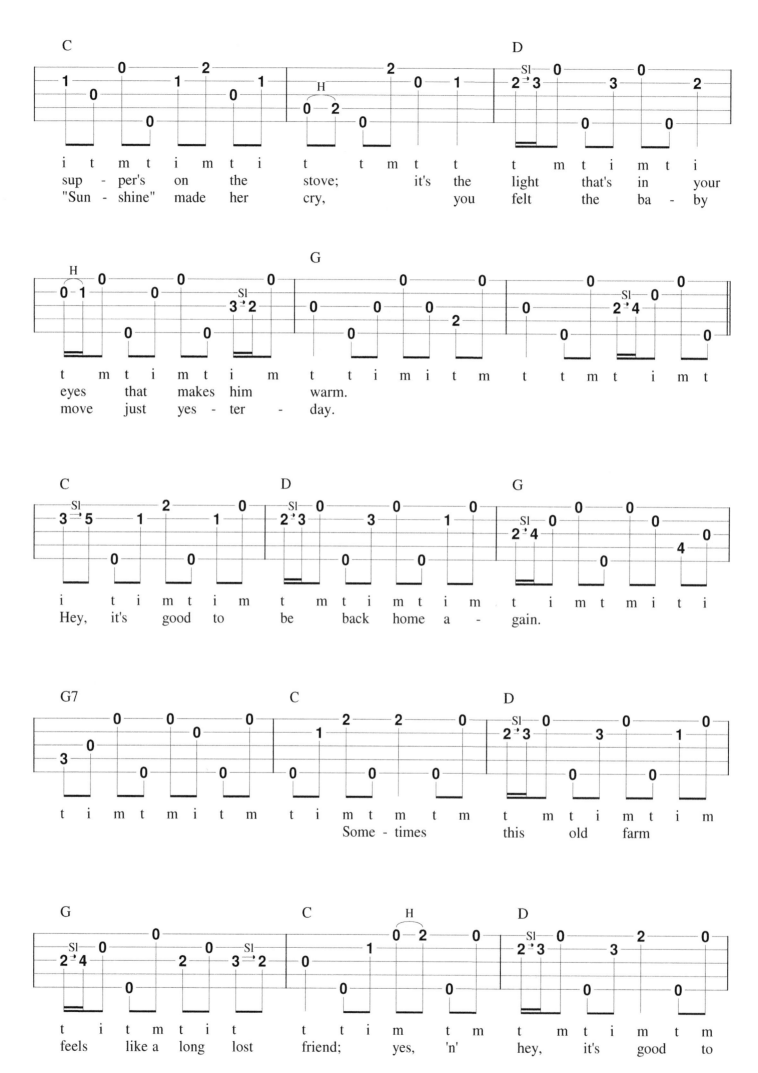

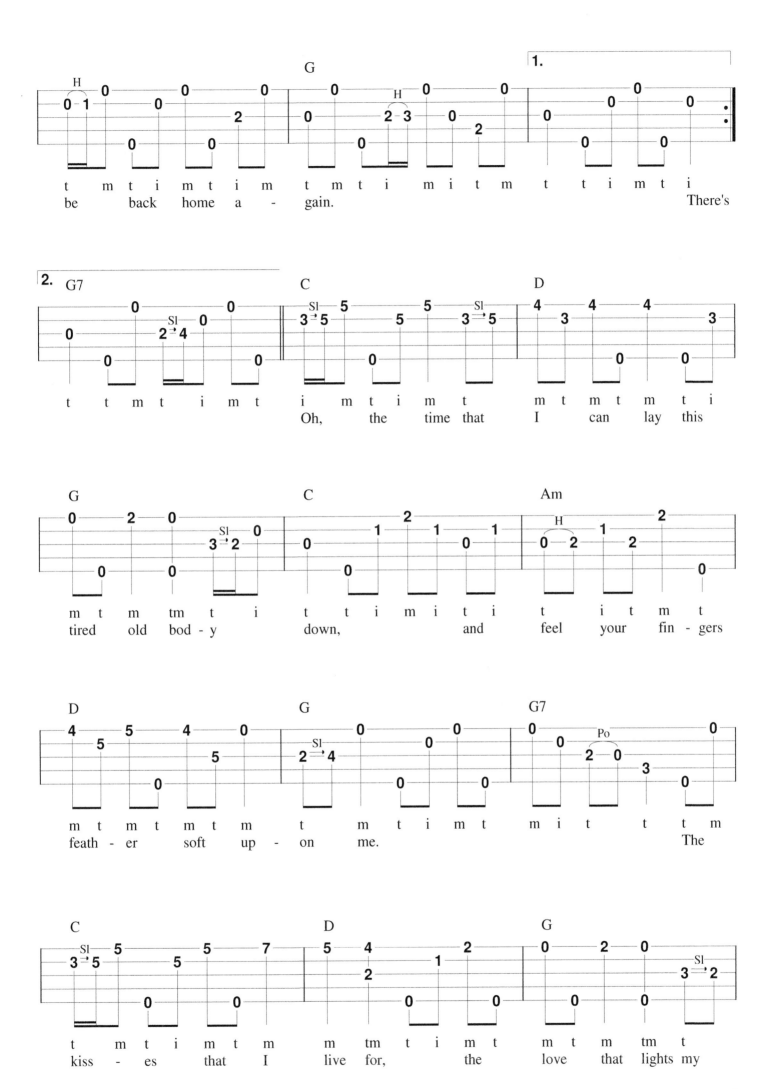

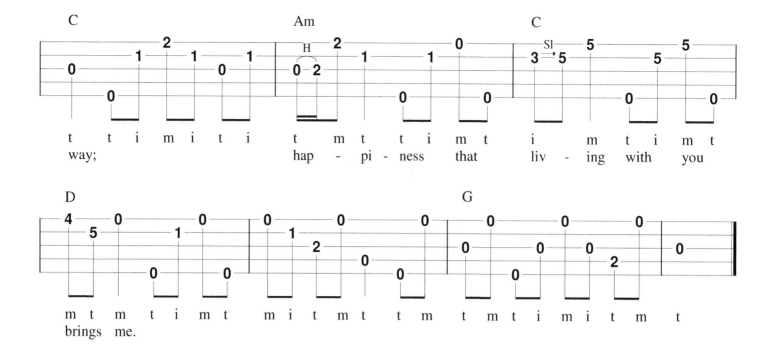

4. It's the sweetest thing I know of, just spending time with you;
   It's the little things that makes a house a home.
   Like a fire softly burning, and supper on the stove,
   The light in your eyes that makes me warm.

   Chorus:

   Hey, it's good to be back home again (yes it is).
   Sometimes this old farm feels like a long lost friend;
   Yes, 'n' hey, it's good to be back home again.

   Repeat Chorus

   Repeat last line of Chorus

FLY AWAY

Words and Music by
John Denver

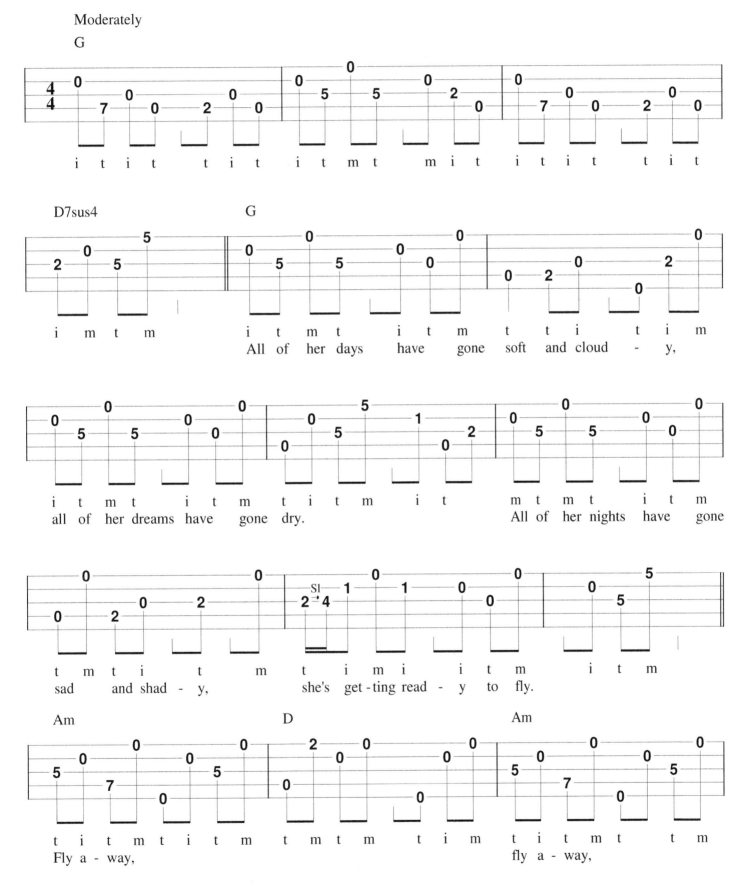

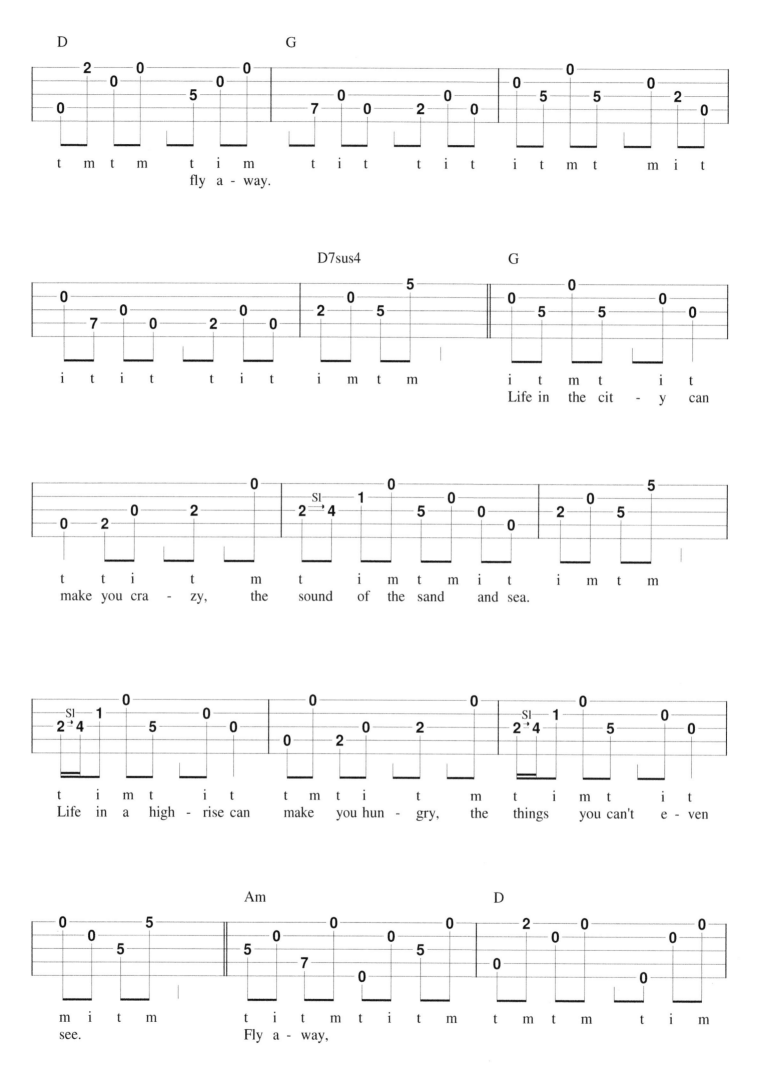

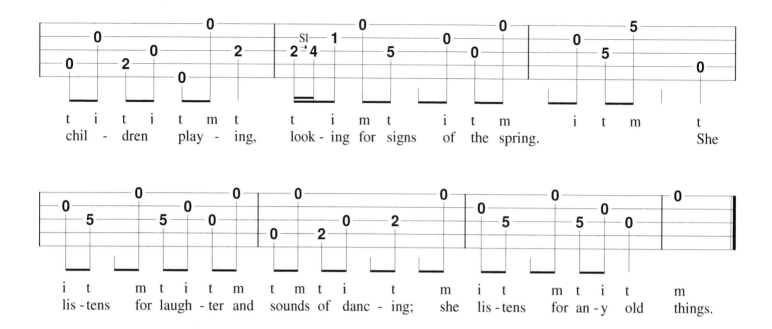

t i t i t m t   t i m t   i t m   i t m   t
chil - dren play - ing,   look - ing for signs   of the spring.   She

i t   m t i t m   t m t i   t   m i t   m t i t   m
lis - tens   for laugh - ter and   sounds of danc - ing;   she lis - tens   for an - y old   things.

Repeat Refrain:

Fly away, fly away, fly away.

Repeat Bridge:

In this whole world nobody is lonely as she.
There's nowhere to go and there's nowhere she'd rather be.

FOLLOW ME

Words and Music by
John Denver

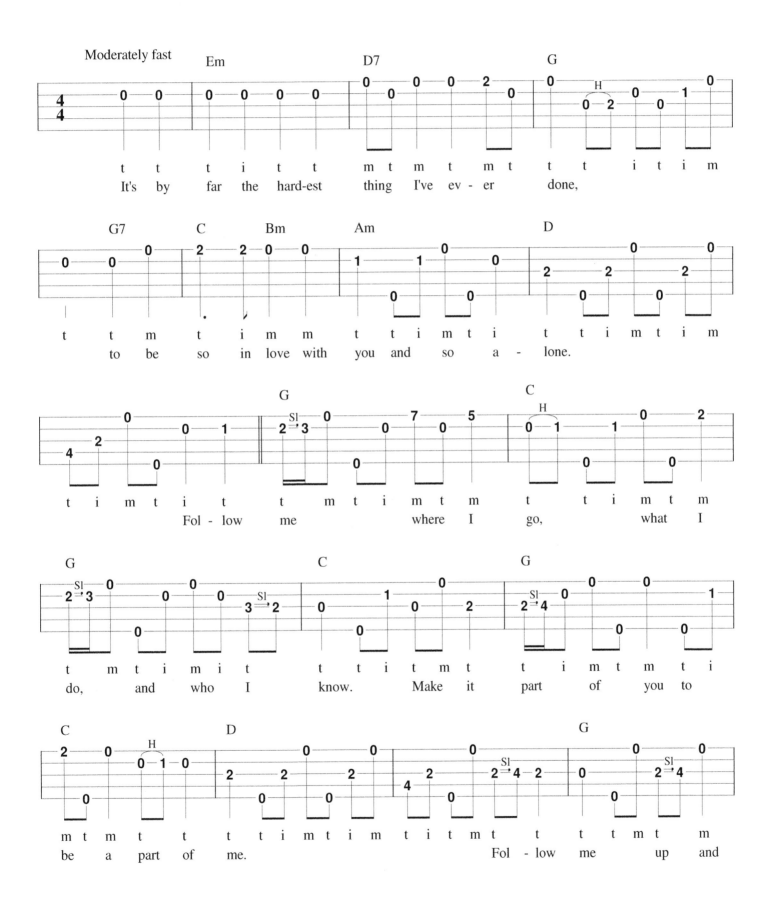

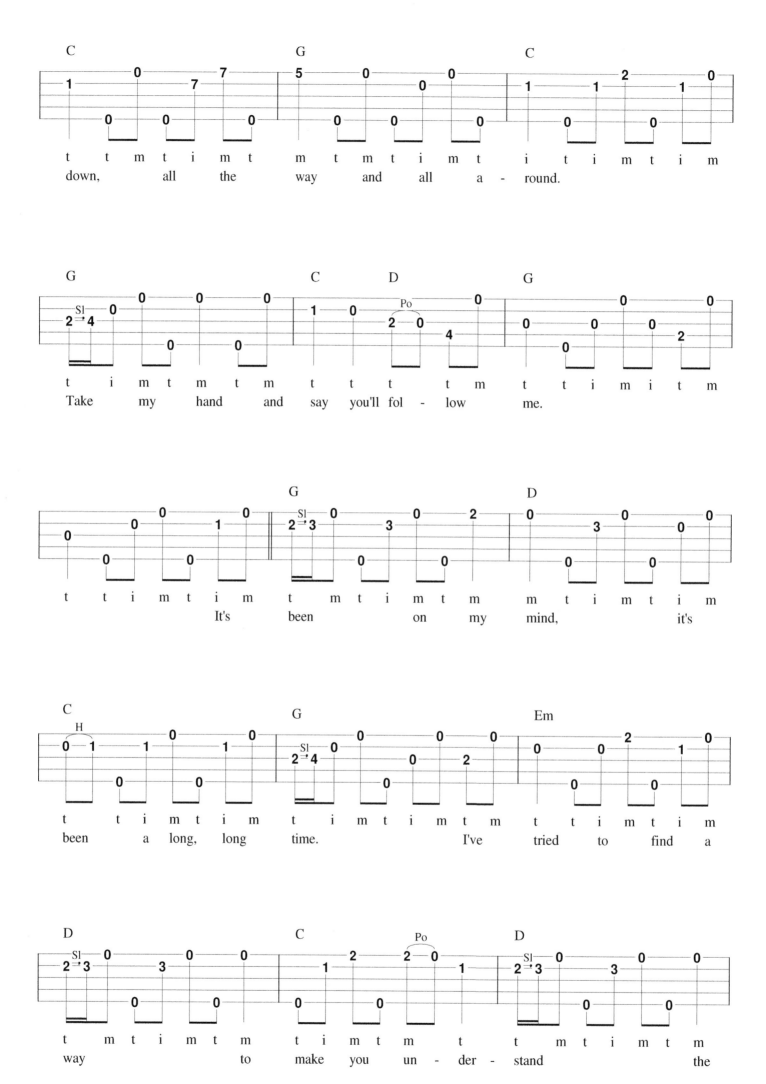

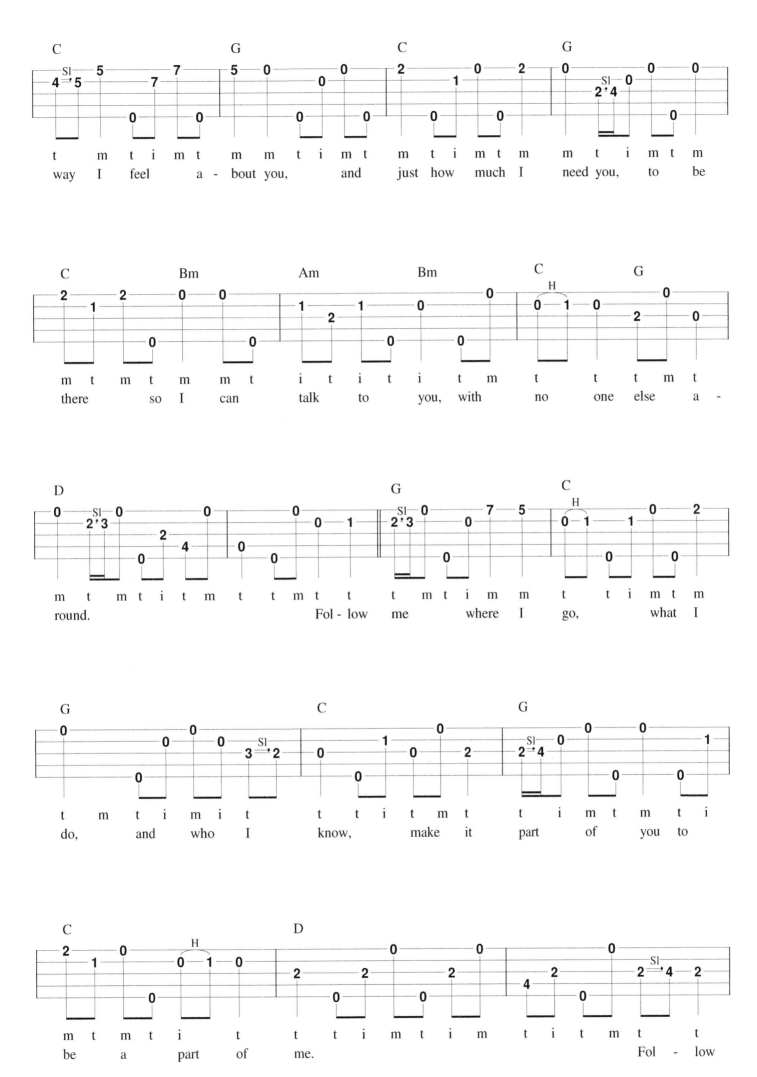

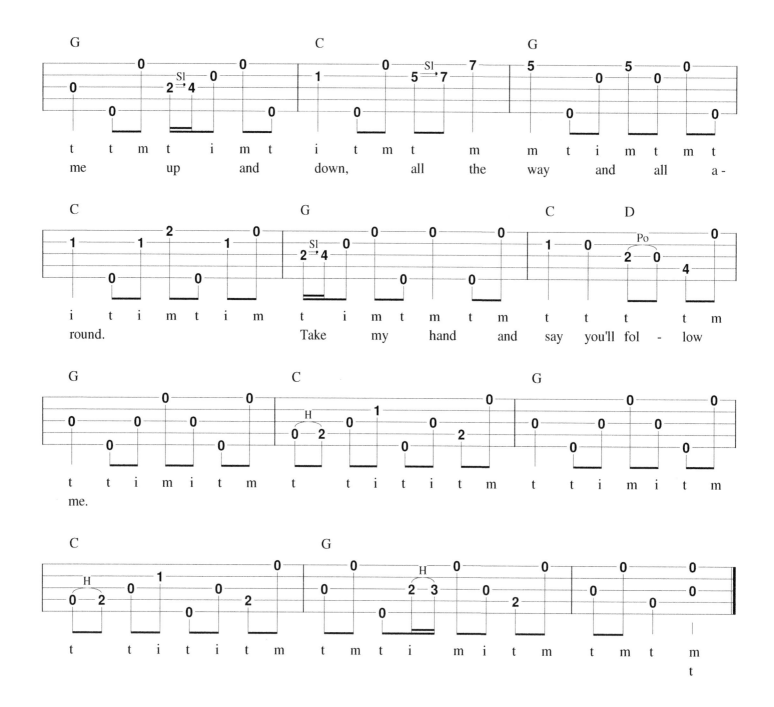

2. You see, I'd like to share my life with you and show you things I've seen,
   Places that I'm going to, places where I've been,
   To have you there beside me, and never be alone,
   And all the time that you're with me, we will be at home.

   to Chorus.

FOR BABY
(For Bobbie)

Words and Music by
John Denver

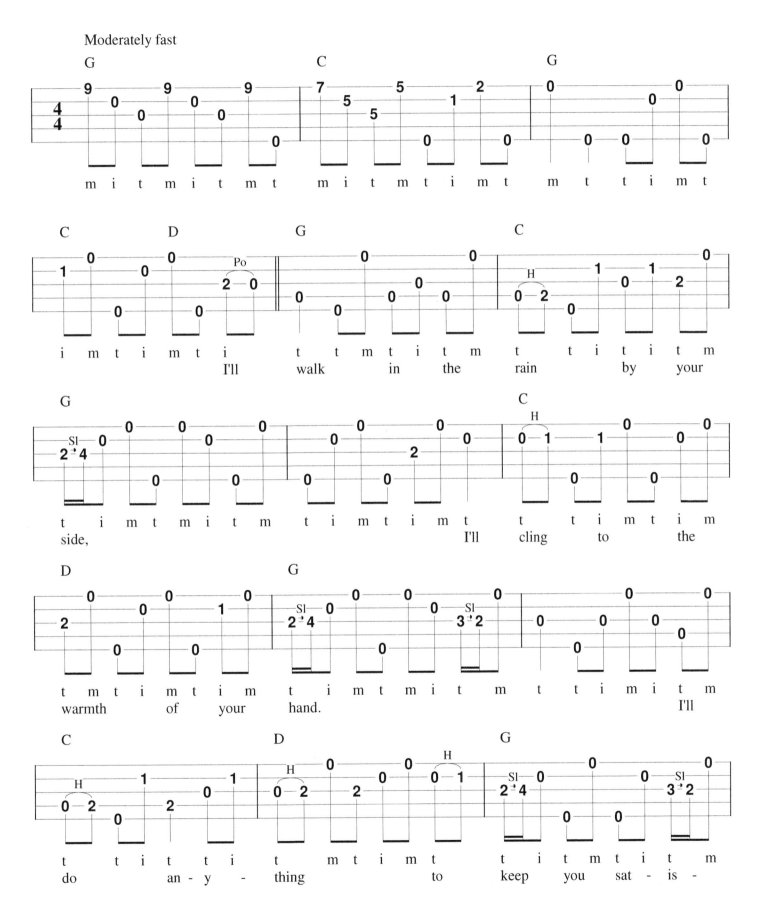

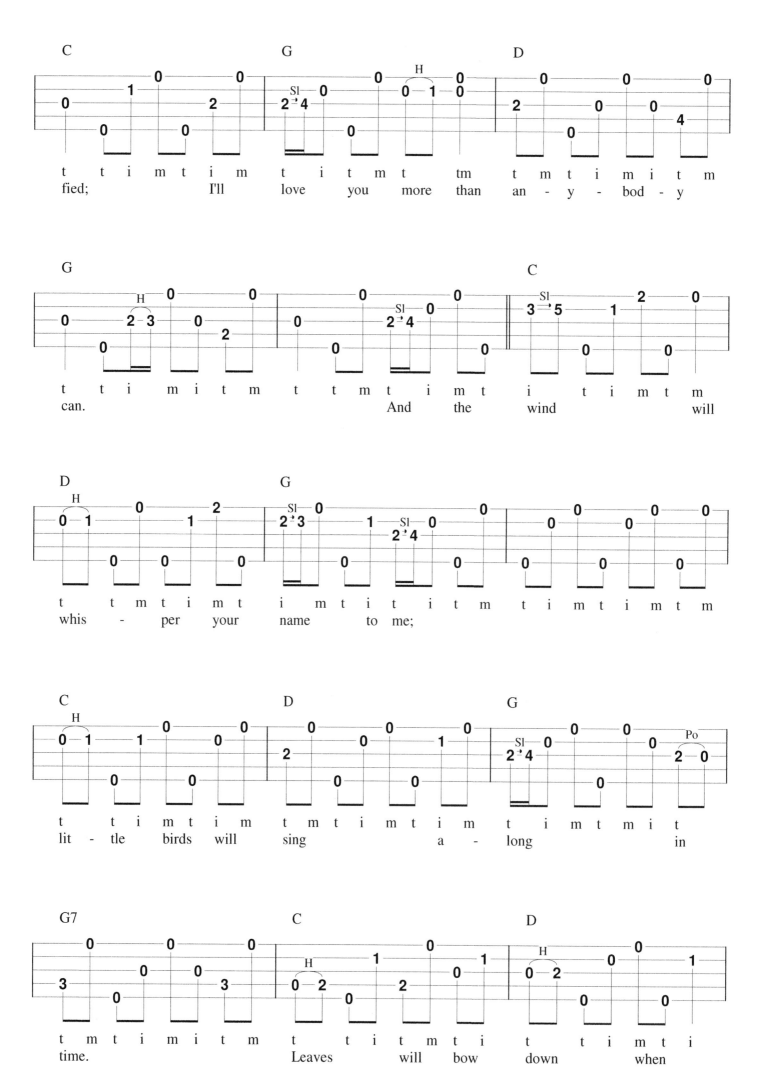

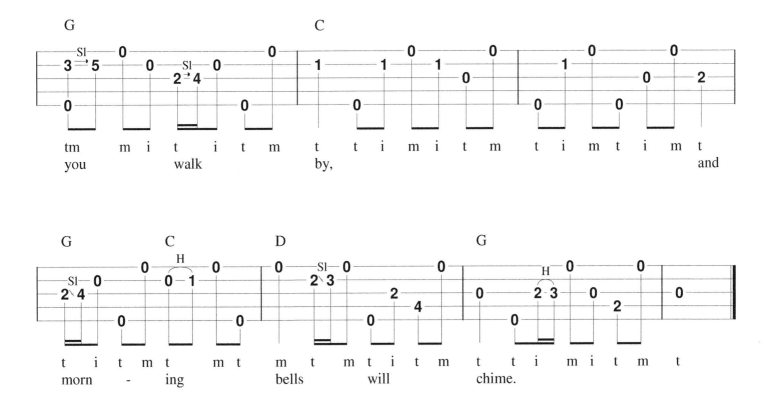

2. I'll be there when you're feelin' down
   To kiss away the tears if you cry.
   I'll share with you all the happiness I've found,
   A reflection of the love in your eyes.

   Chorus:

   And I'll sing you the songs of the rainbow,
   A whisper of the joy that is mine.
   And leaves will bow down when you walk by,
   And morning bells will chime.

3. I'll walk in the rain by your side,
   I'll cling to the warmth of your tiny hand.
   I'll do anything to help understand,
   And I'll love you more than anybody can.

   Chorus:

   And the wind will whisper your name to me,
   Little birds will sing along in time.
   Leaves will bow down when you walk by,
   And morning bells will chime.

GARDEN SONG

Words and Music by
Dave Mallett

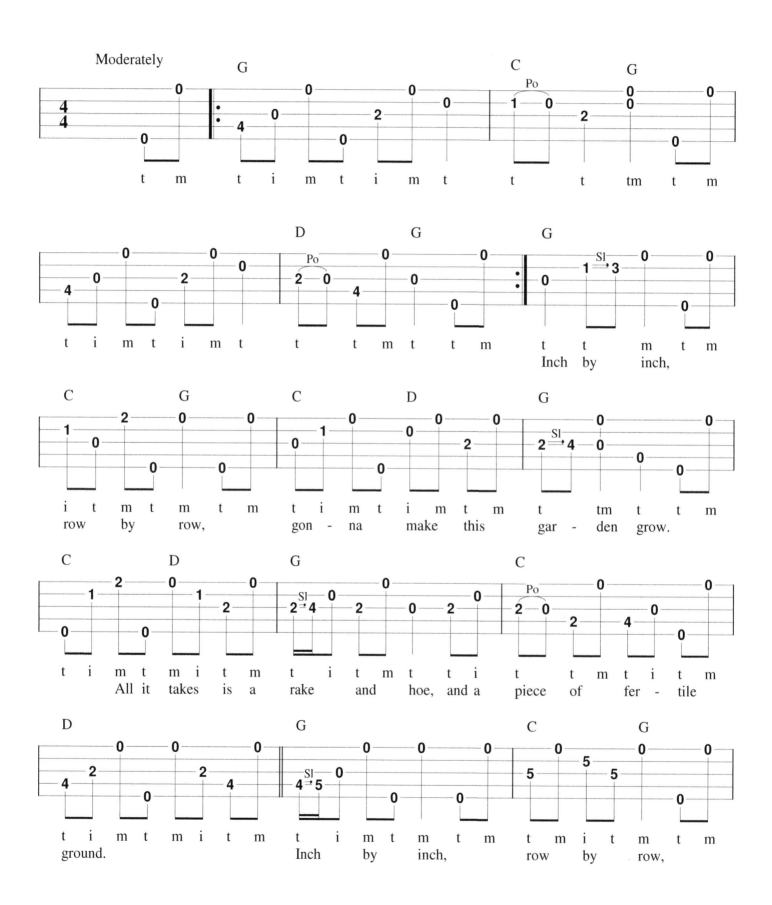

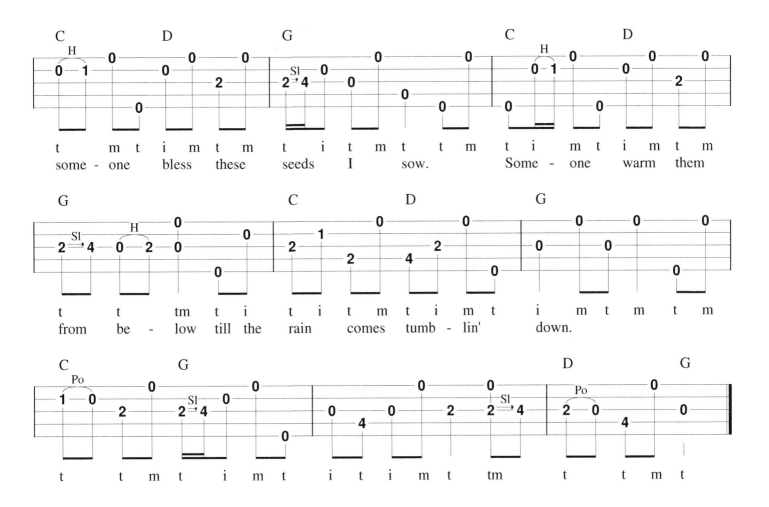

3. Pullin' weeds and pickin' stones,
   Man is made of dreams and bones.
   Feel the need to grow my own,
   'Cause the time is close at hand.

4. Rainful rain, sun and rain,
   Find my way in nature's chain.
   Tune my body and my brain,
   To the music from the land.

5. Plant your rows straight and long,
   Temper them with prayer and song.
   Mother Earth will make you strong
   If you give her love and care.

6. Old crow watchin' hungrily
   From his perch in yonder tree.
   In my garden I'm as free
   As that feathered thief up there.

GOODBYE AGAIN

Words and Music by
John Denver

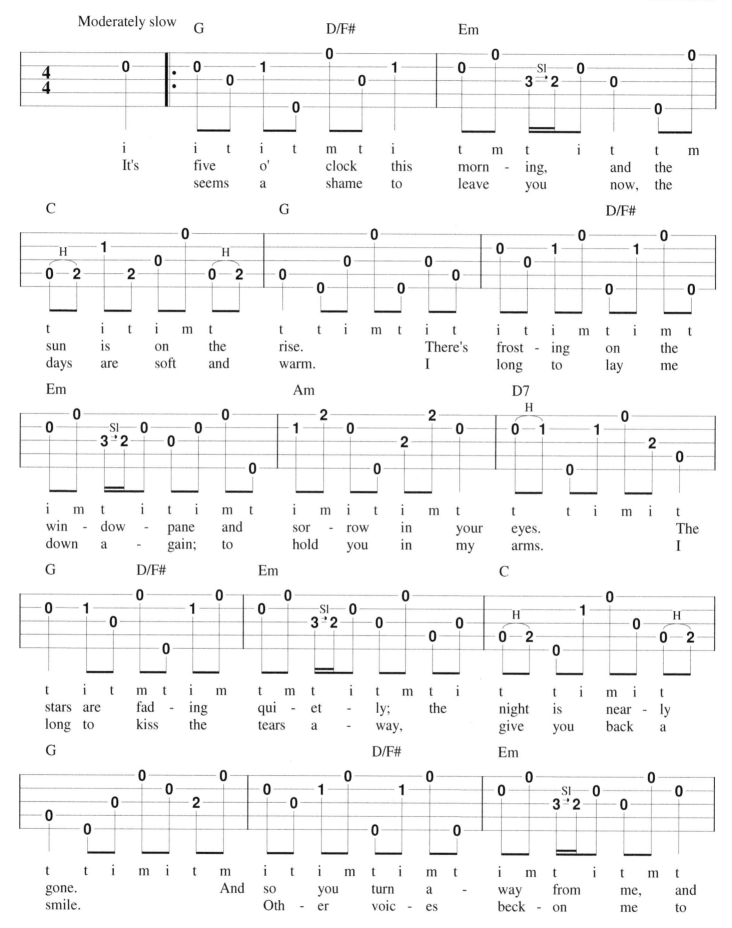

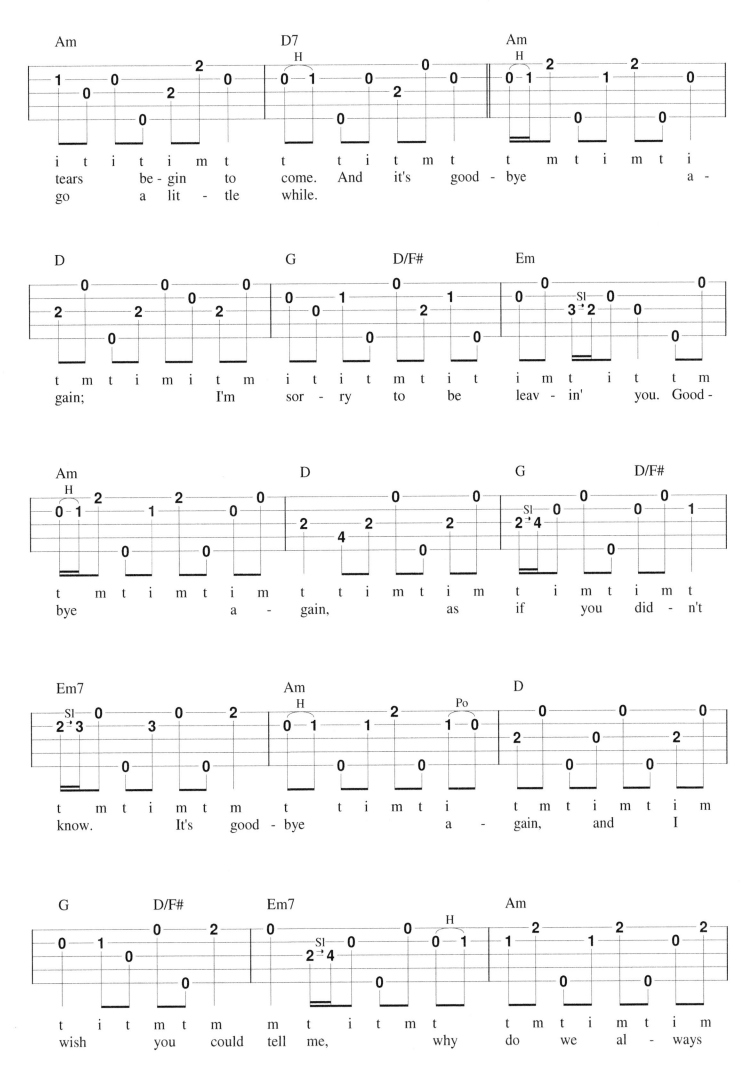

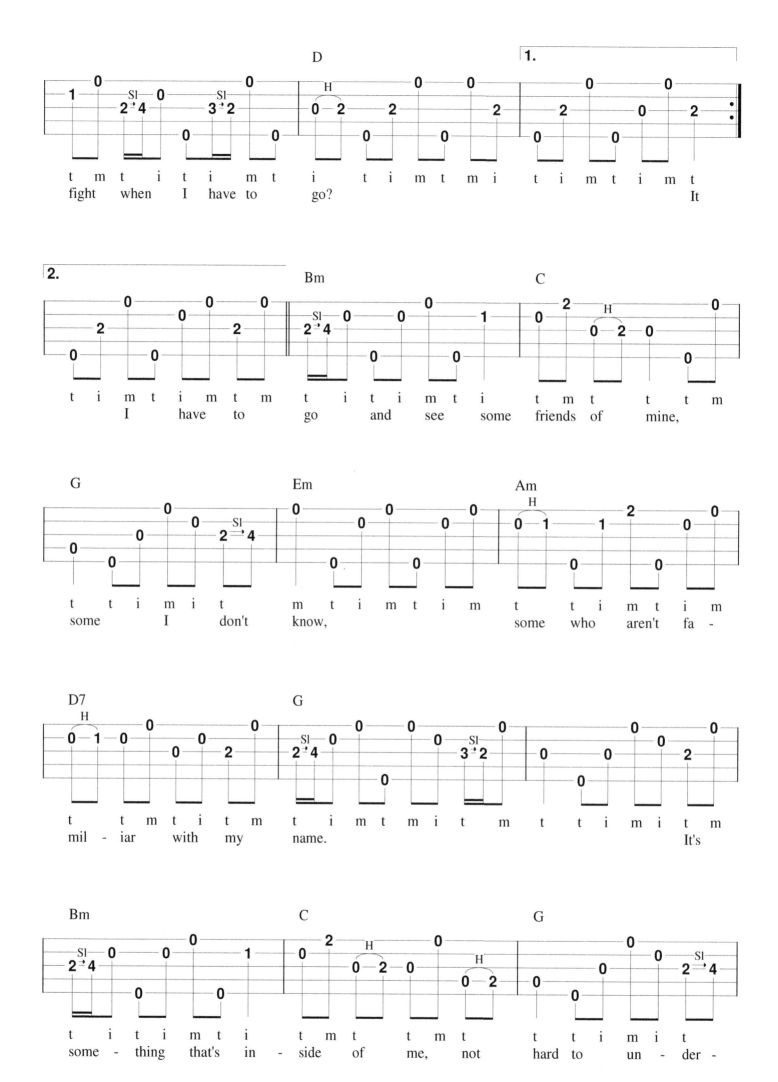

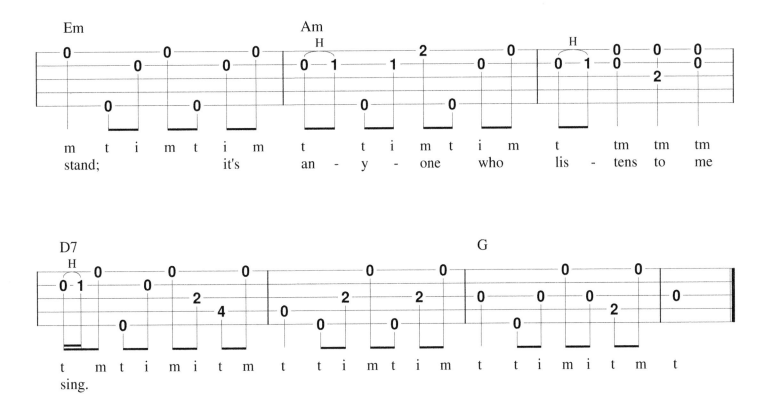

m t i m t i m   t   t i m t i m   t   tm tm tm

stand;   it's   an - y - one who   lis - tens to me

t   m t i m i t m   t   t i m t i m   t   t i m i t m   t

sing.

3. And if your hours are empty now, who am I to blame?
   You'd think if I were always here, our love would be the same.
   As it is, the time we have is worth the time alone.
   And lying by your side is the greatest peace I've ever known.

   Chorus:

   But it's goodbye again; I'm sorry to be leavin' you.
   Goodbye again, as if you didn't know.
   It's goodbye again, and I wish you could tell me,
   Why do we always fight when I have to go?

GRANDMA'S FEATHER BED

Words and Music by
Jim Connor

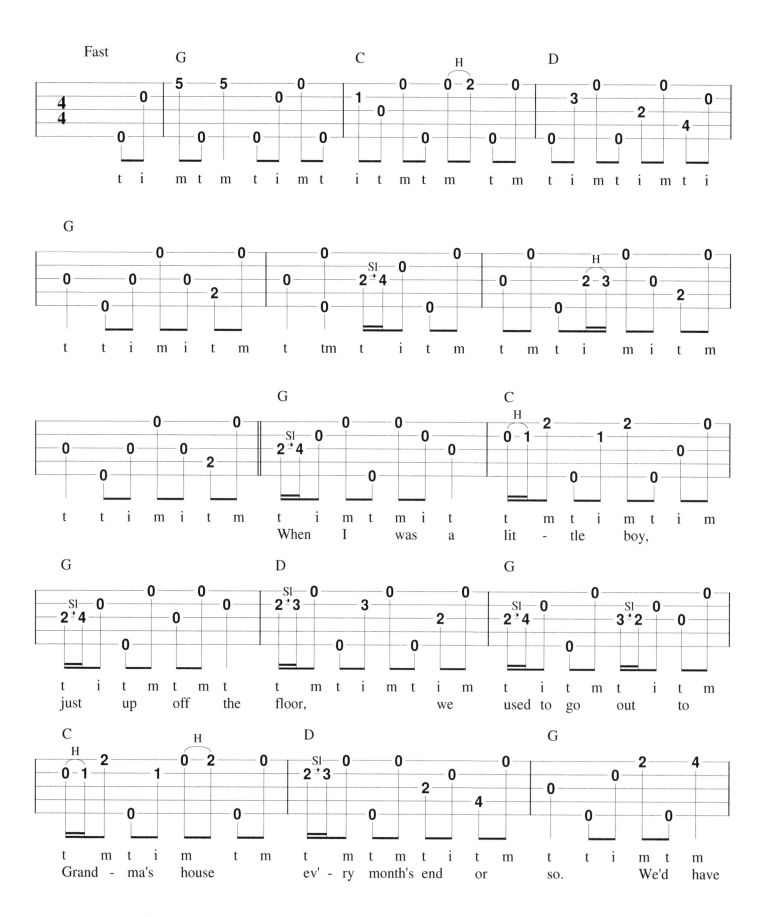

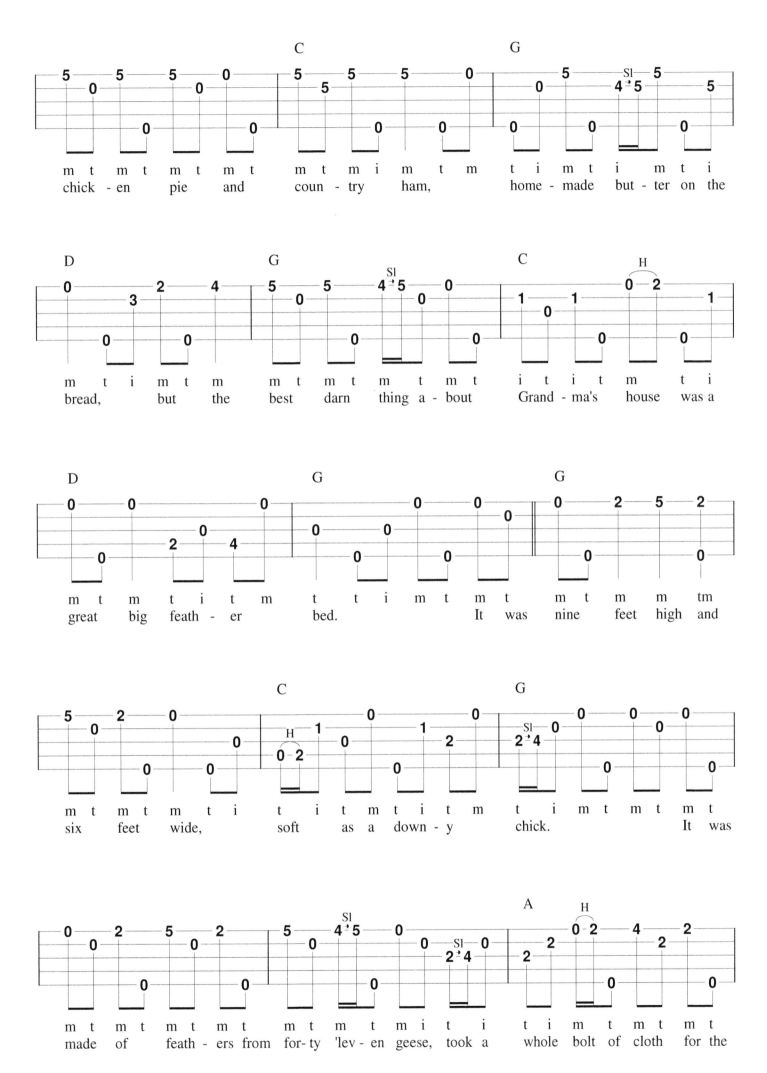

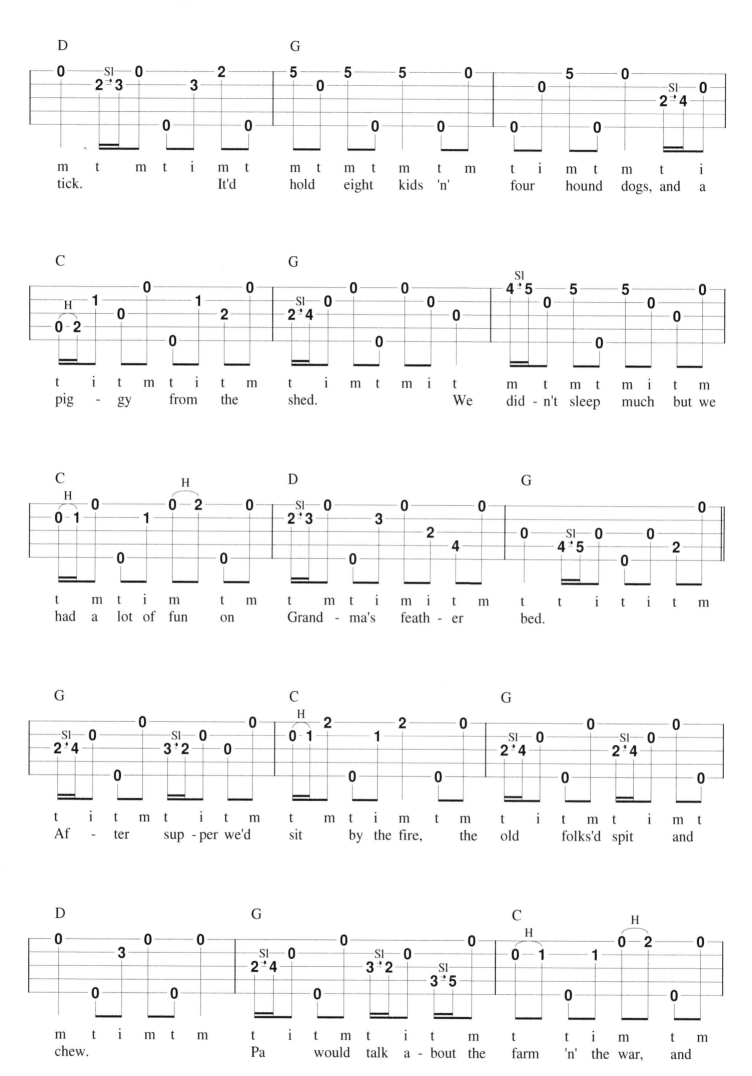

3. Well I love my ma and I love my pa, I love Granny and Grandpa too,
   I been fishin' with my uncle, I rassled with my cousin, I even kissed Aunt Lou....ewww!
   But if I ever had to make a choice, I guess it oughta be said
   That I'd trade 'em all plus the gal down the road for Grandma's feather bed.

   Repeat Chorus

I GUESS HE'D RATHER BE IN COLORADO

Words and Music by
Bill Danoff and Taffy Nivert Danoff

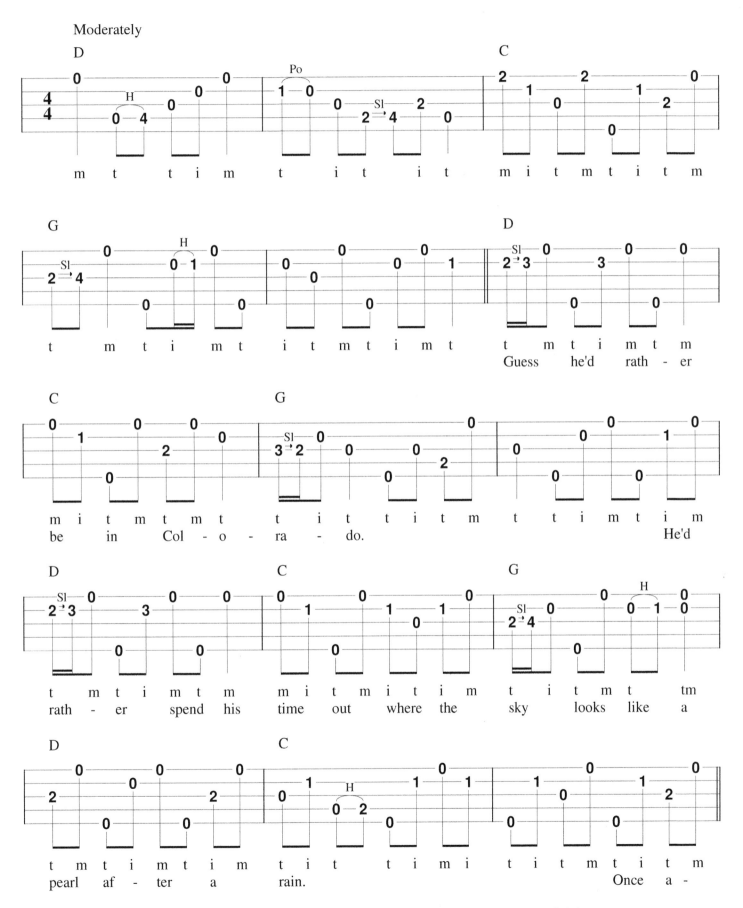

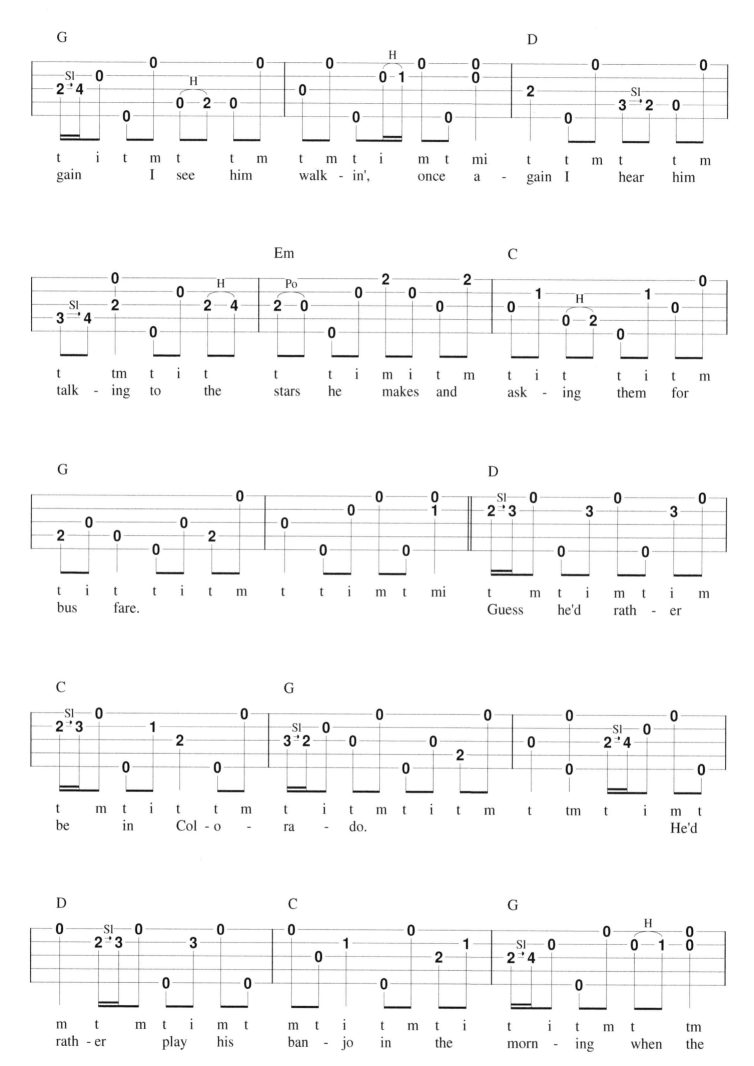

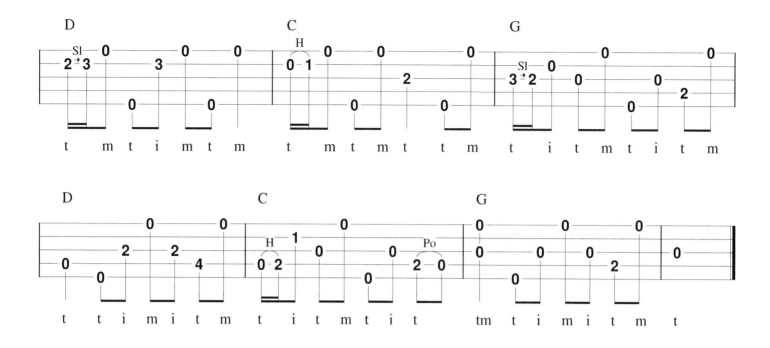

3. I guess he'd rather be in Colorado.
   I guess he'd rather work out where the only thing you earn is what you spend.
   In the end up in his office, in the end a quiet cough is all he has to show.
   He lives in New York City.

I'M SORRY

Words and Music by
John Denver

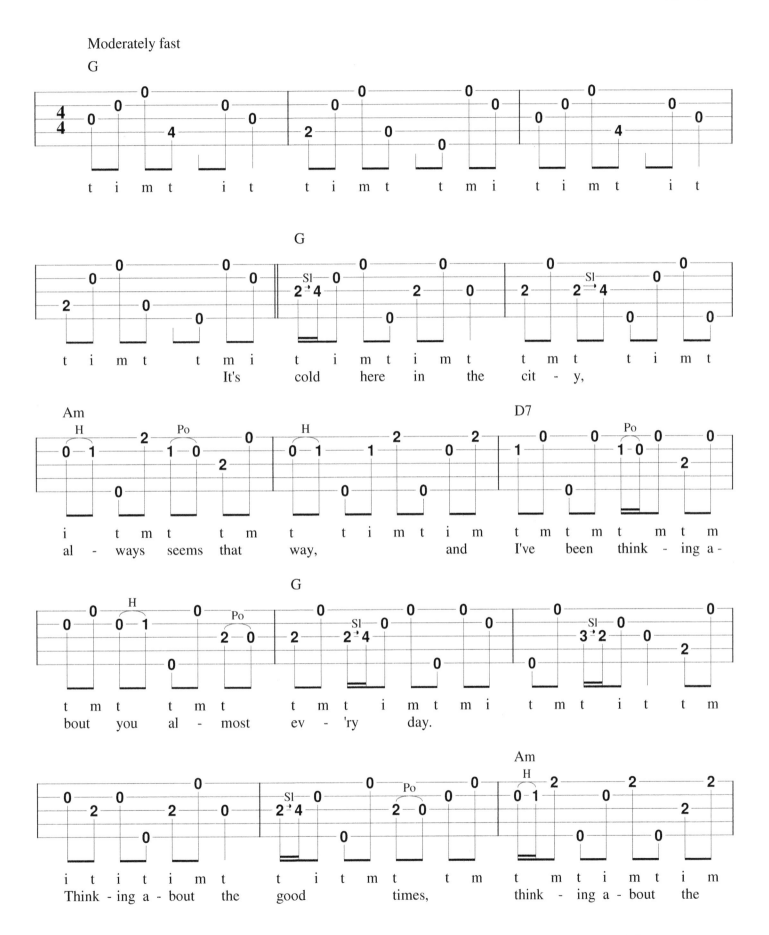

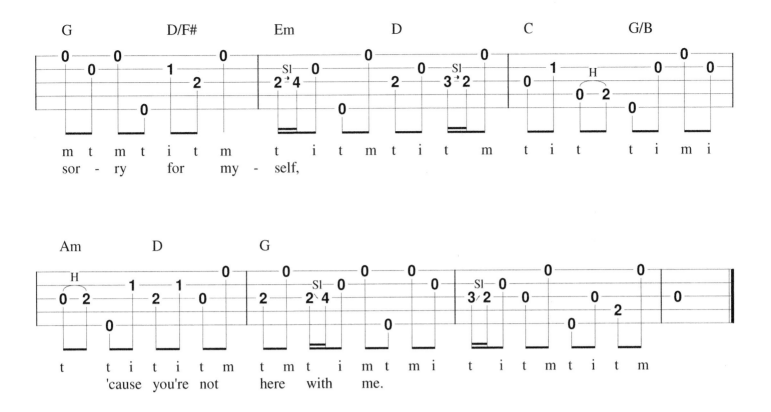

sor - ry   for   my - self,

'cause you're not   here   with   me.

2. Our friends all ask about you; I say you're doing fine,
   I expect to hear from you almost anytime.
   They all know I'm crying, I can't sleep at night;
   They all know I'm dying down deep inside.

   Second Refrain:

   I'm sorry for all the lies I told you;
   I'm sorry for the things I didn't say.
   More than anything else, I'm sorry for myself.
   I can't believe you went away.

   Third Refrain:

   I'm sorry if I took some things for granted;
   I'm sorry for the chains I put on you.
   More than anything else, I'm sorry for myself
   For living without you.

LEAVING ON A JET PLANE

Words and Music by
John Denver

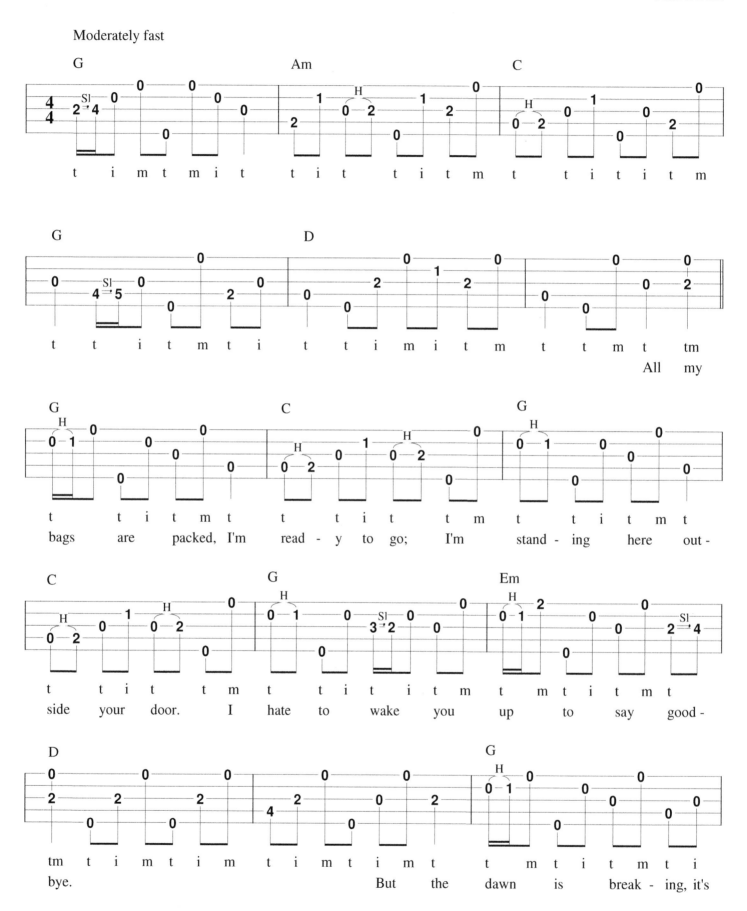

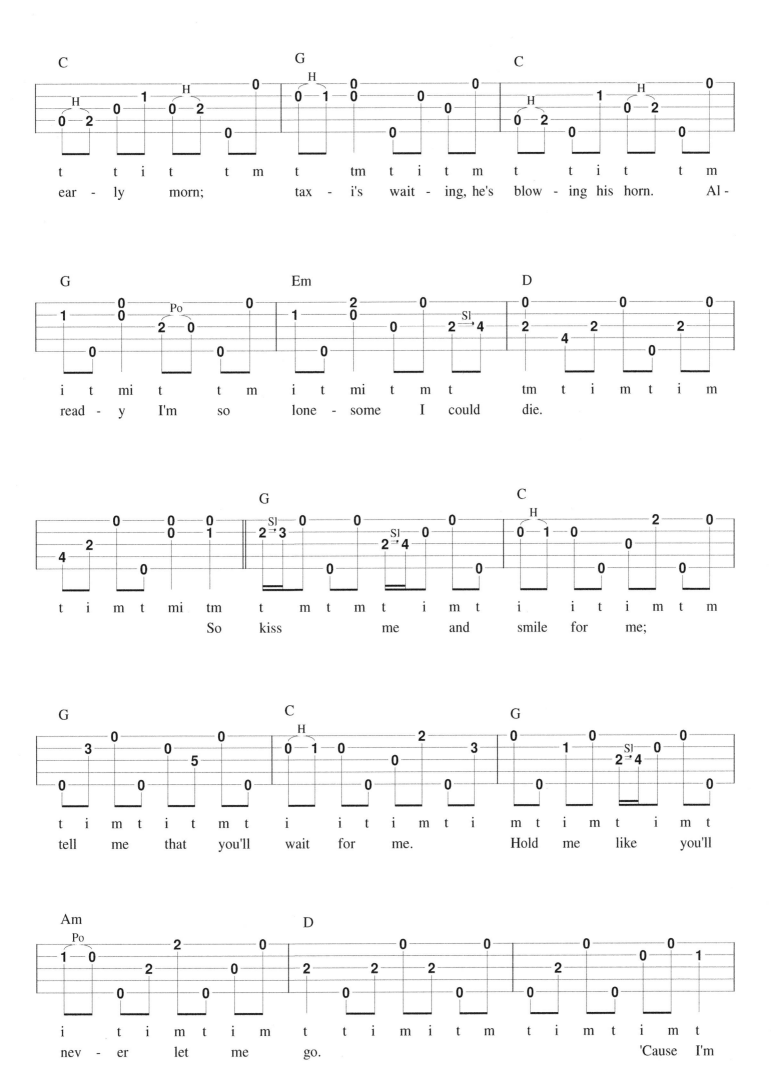

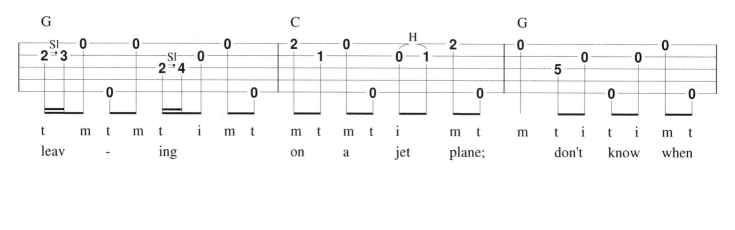

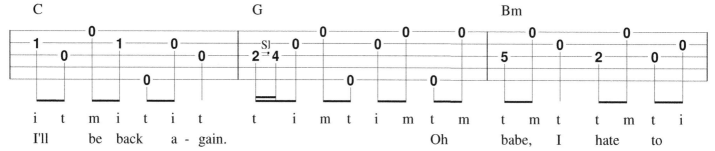

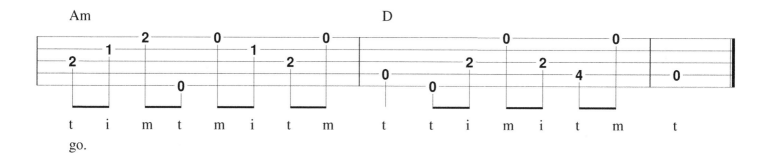

2. There's so many times I've let you down, so many times I've played around.
   I tell you now, they don't mean a thing.
   Every place I go, I'll think of you; every song I sing, I'll sing for you.
   When I come back, I'll bring your wedding ring.

   Chorus

   So kiss me and smile for me; tell me that you'll wait for me.
   Hold me like you'll never let me go.
   'Cause I'm leaving on a jet plane; don't know when I'll be back again.
   Oh babe, I hate to go.

3. Now the time has come to leave you; one more time let me kiss you.
   Close your eyes and I'll be on my way.
   Dream about the days to come, when I won't have to leave alone,
   About the times, I won't have to say:

   Repeat Chorus

PERHAPS LOVE

Words and Music by
John Denver

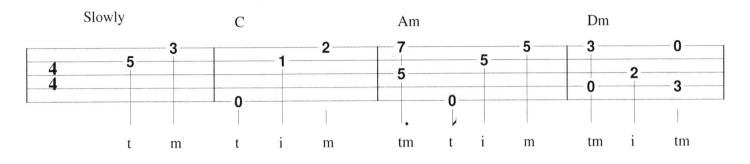

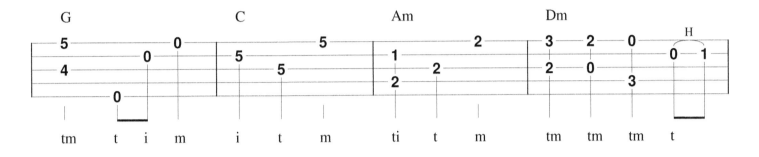

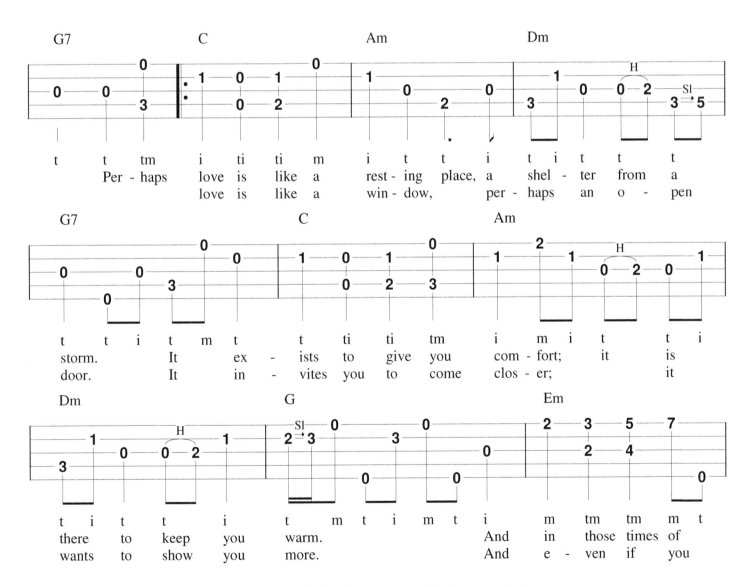

Per - haps love is like a rest - ing place, a shel - ter from a
love is like a win - dow, per - haps an o - pen

storm. It ex - ists to give you com - fort; it is
door. It in - vites you to come clos - er; it

there to keep you warm. And in those times of
wants to show you more. And e - ven if you

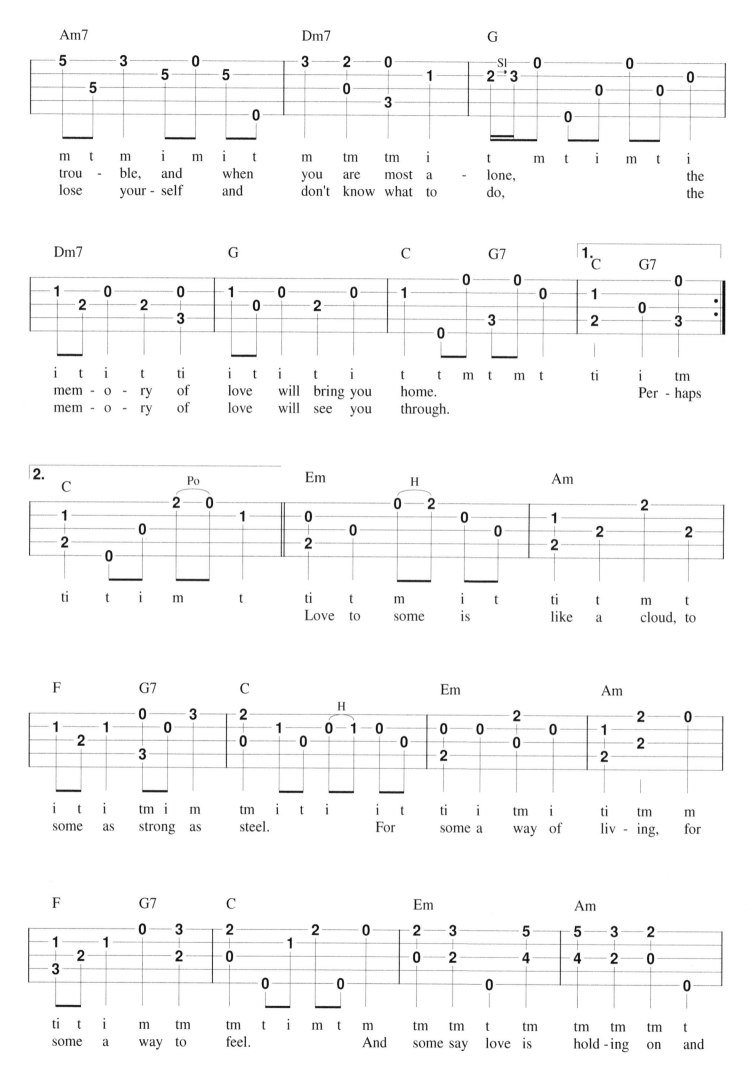

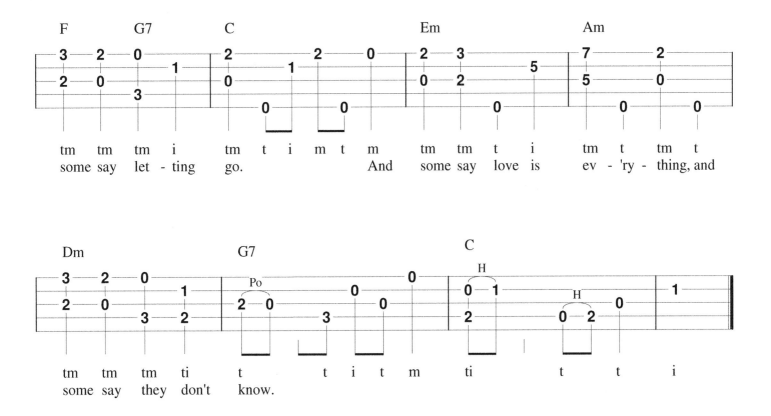

F	G7	C				Em		Am	

tm tm tm i   tm t i m t m   tm tm t i   tm t tm t

some say let - ting go.   And some say love is   ev - 'ry - thing, and

Dm	G7	C

tm tm tm ti   t t i t m   ti t t i

some say they don't know.

3. Perhaps love is like the ocean, full of conflict, full of pain.
   Like a fire when it's cold outside, thunder when it rains.
   If I should live forever, and all my dreams come true,
   My memories of love will be of you.

POEMS, PRAYERS AND PROMISES

Words and Music by
John Denver

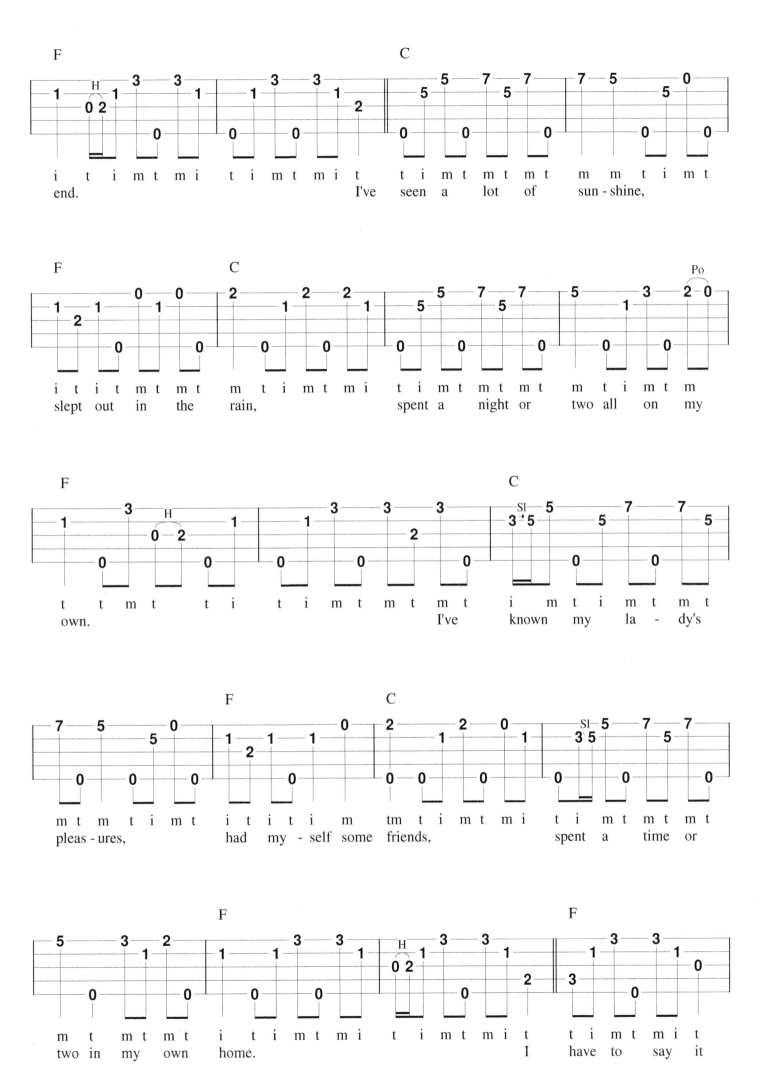

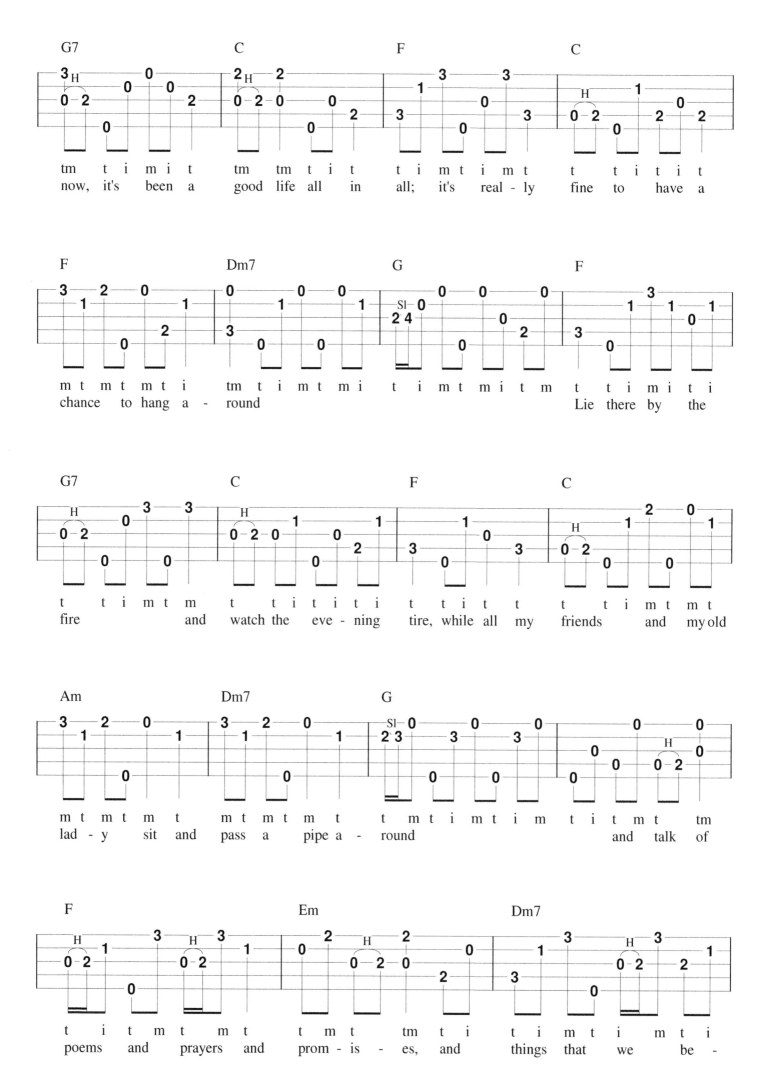

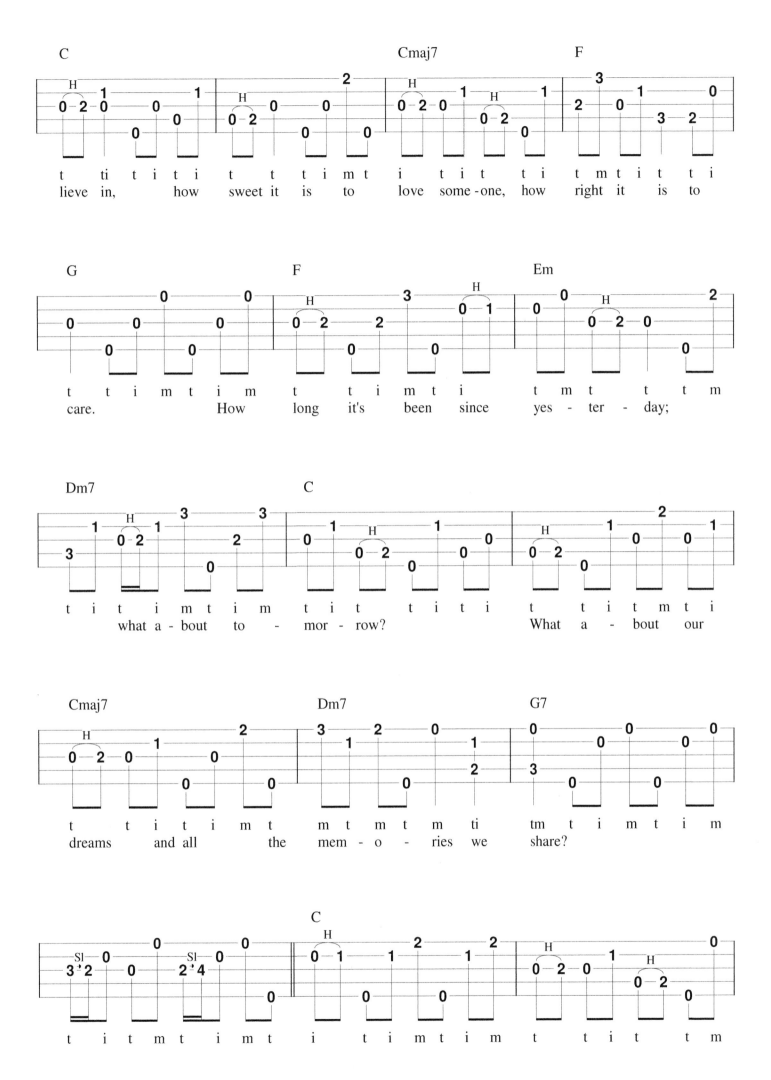

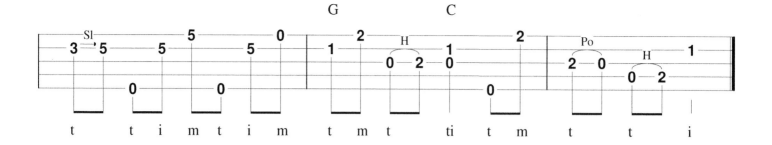

3. The days, they pass so quickly; now the nights are seldom long.
   Time around me whispers when it's cold.
   Changes somehow frighten me; still I have to smile.
   It turns me on to think of growing old.

4. For though my life's been good to me, there's still so much to do,
   So many things my mind has never known.
   I'd like to raise a family; I'd like to sail away,
   And dance across the mountains on the moon.

   Bridge:

   I have to say it now, it's been a good life all in all;
   It's really fine to have a chance to hang around.
   Lie there by the fire and watch the evening tire,
   While all my friends and my old lady sit and pass the pipe around

   Refrain:

   And talk of poems and prayers and promises, and things that we believe in,
   How sweet it is to love someone, how right it is to care.
   How long it's been since yesterday; what about tomorrow?
   What about our dreams and all the memories we share?

RHYMES AND REASONS

Words and Music by
John Denver

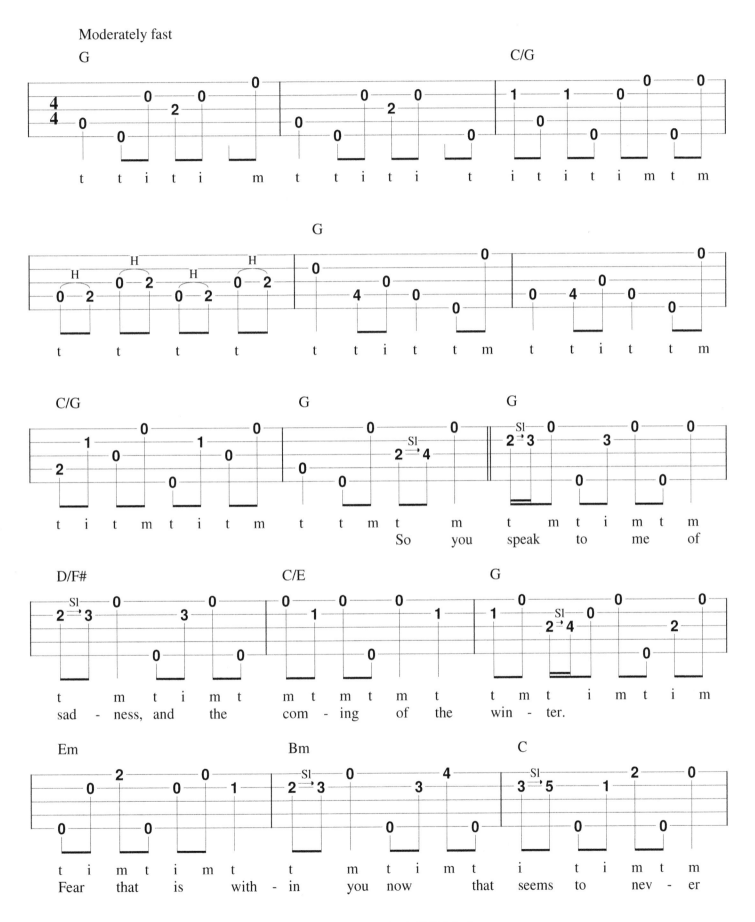

Moderately fast

So you speak to me of sad-ness, and the com-ing of the win-ter. Fear that is with-in you now that seems to nev-er

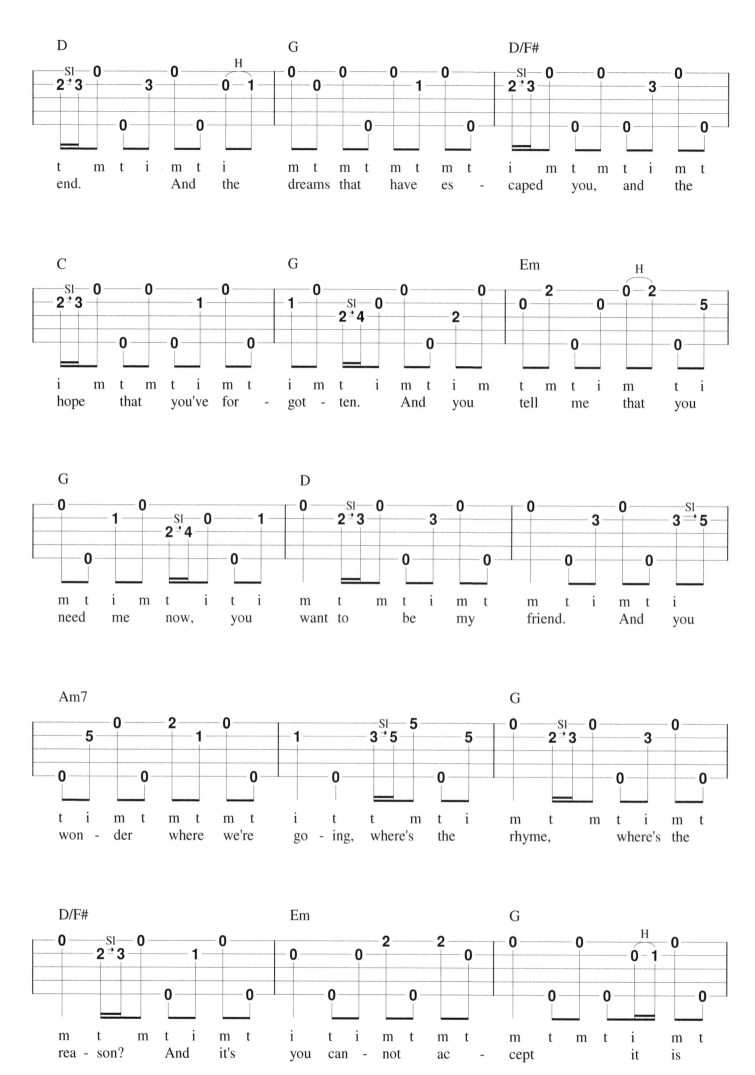

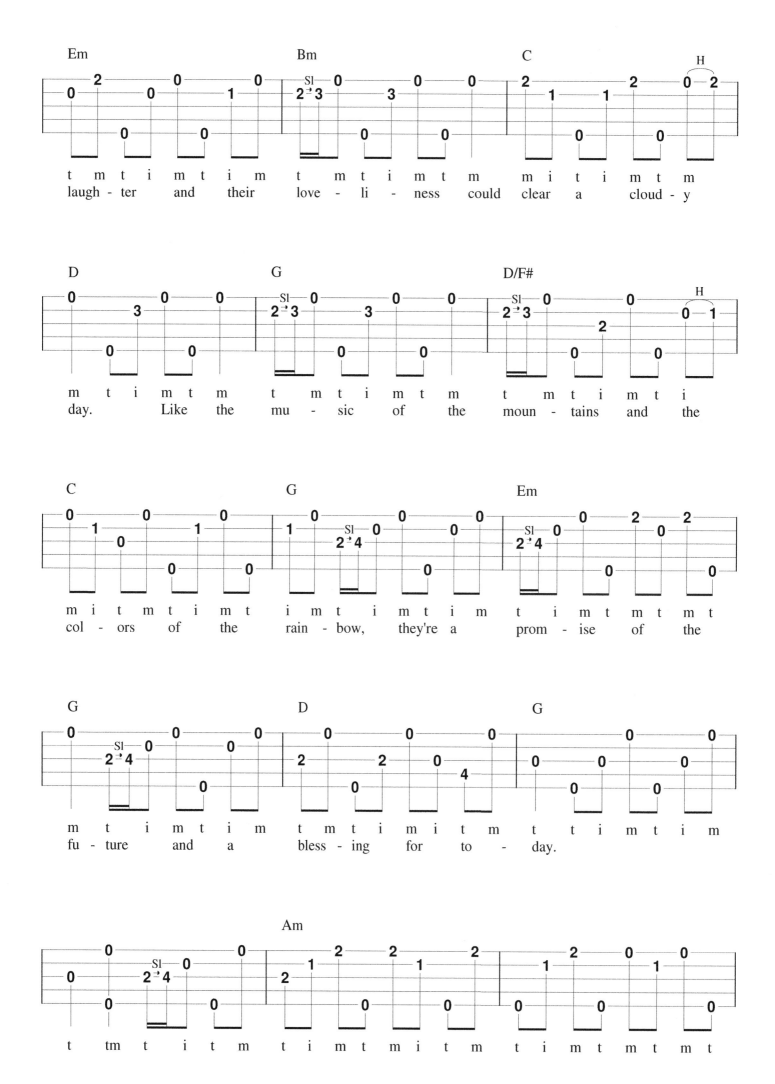

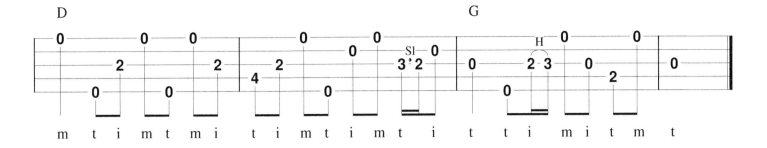

3. Though the cities start to crumble and the towers fall around us,
   The sun is slowly fading and it's colder than the sea.
   It is written from the desert, to the mountains they shall lead us,
   By the hand and by the heart, they will comfort you and me.
   In their innocence and trusting they will teach us to be free.

4. For the children and the flowers are my sisters and my brothers;
   Their laughter and their loveliness could clear a cloudy day.
   And the song that I am singing is a prayer to non-believers.
   Come and stand beside us; we can find a better way.

ROCKY MOUNTAIN HIGH

Words and Music by
John Denver and Mike Taylor

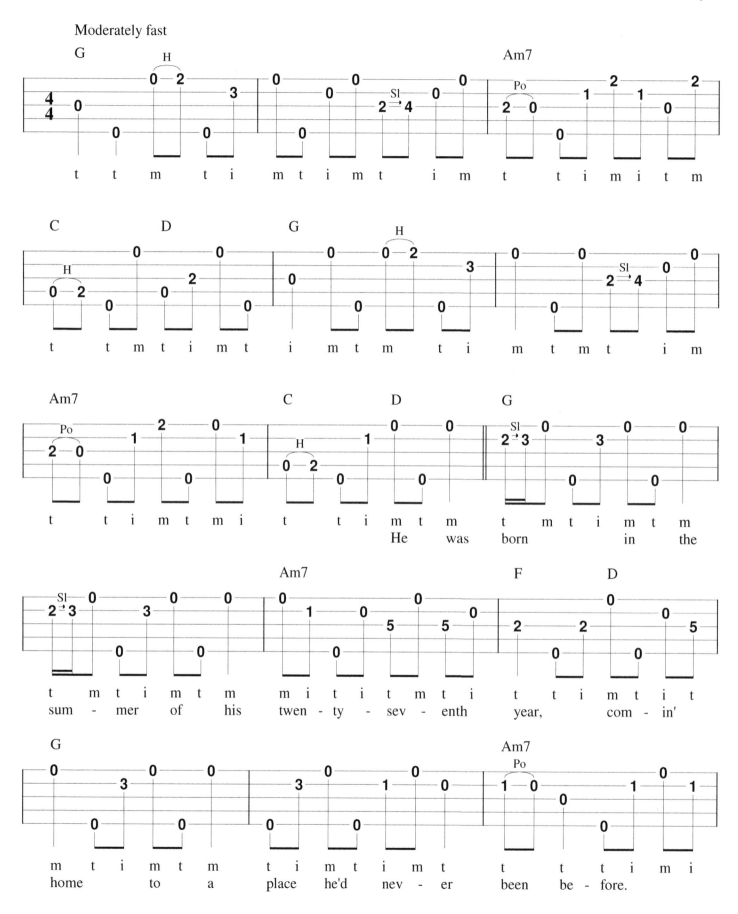

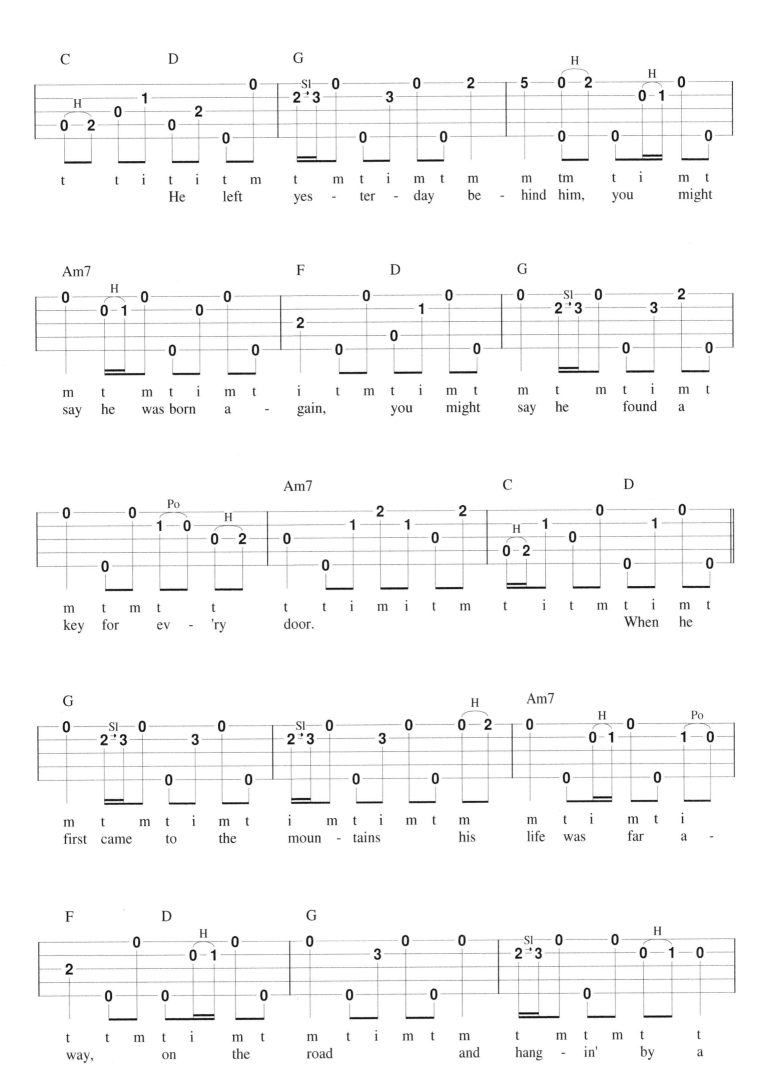

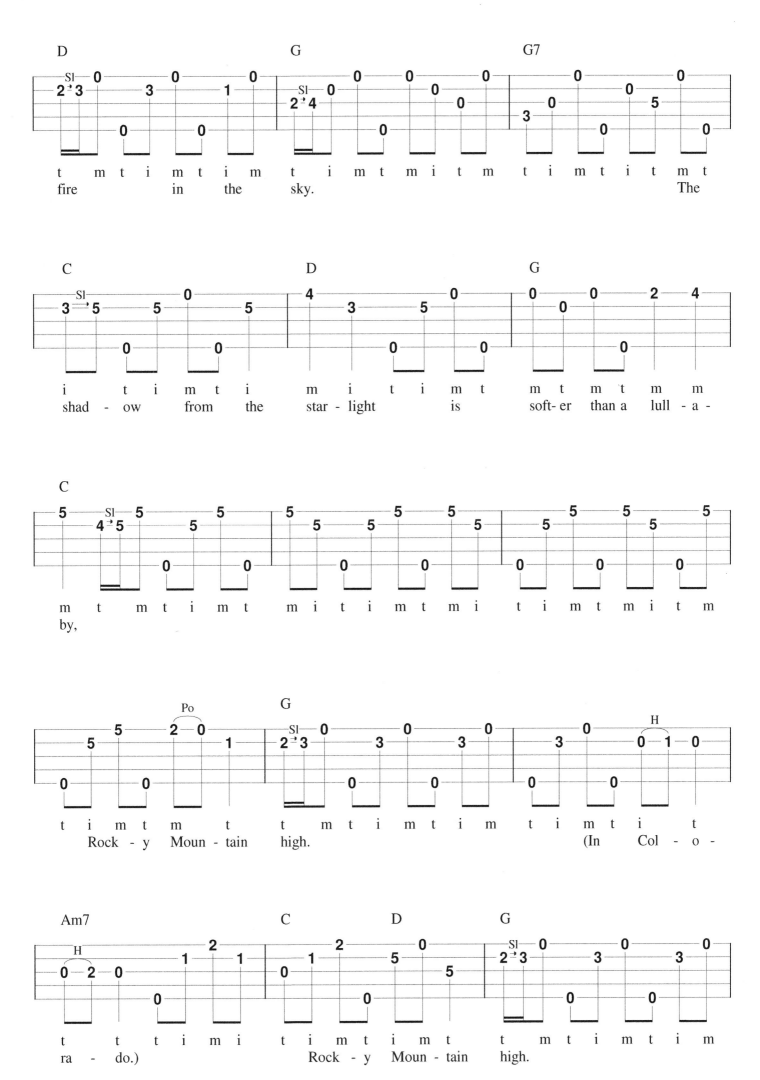

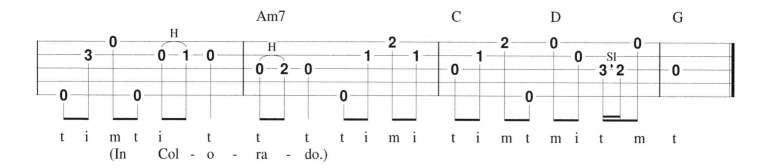

(In Col - o - ra - do.)

3. He climbed cathedral mountains, he saw silver clouds below.
He saw everything as far as you can see.
And they say that he got crazy once and he tried to touch the sun,
And he lost a friend but kept his memory.

4. Now he walks in quiet solitude the forests and the streams,
Seeking grace in every step he takes.
His sight has turned inside himself to try and understand
The serenity of a clear mountain lake.

2nd Chorus:
And the Colorado Rocky Mountain high,
I've seen it rainin' fire in the sky.
You can talk to God and listen to the casual reply,
Rocky Mountain High. (In Colorado.)
Rocky Mountain High. (In Colorado.)

5. Now his life is full of wonder but his heart still knows some fear
Of a simple thing he cannot comprehend.
Why they try to tear the mountains down to bring in a couple more,
More people, more scars upon the land.

3rd Chorus:
And the Colorado Rocky Mountain high,
I've seen it rainin' fire in the sky.
I know he'd be a poorer man if he never saw an eagle fly.
Rocky Mountain High.

4th Chorus:
It's a Colorado Rocky Mountain high.
I've seen it rainin' fire in the sky.
Friends around the campfire and everybody's high.
Rocky Mountain High. (In Colorado.)

SUNSHINE ON MY SHOULDERS

Words by
John Denver

Music by
John Denver, Mike Taylor
and Dick Kniss

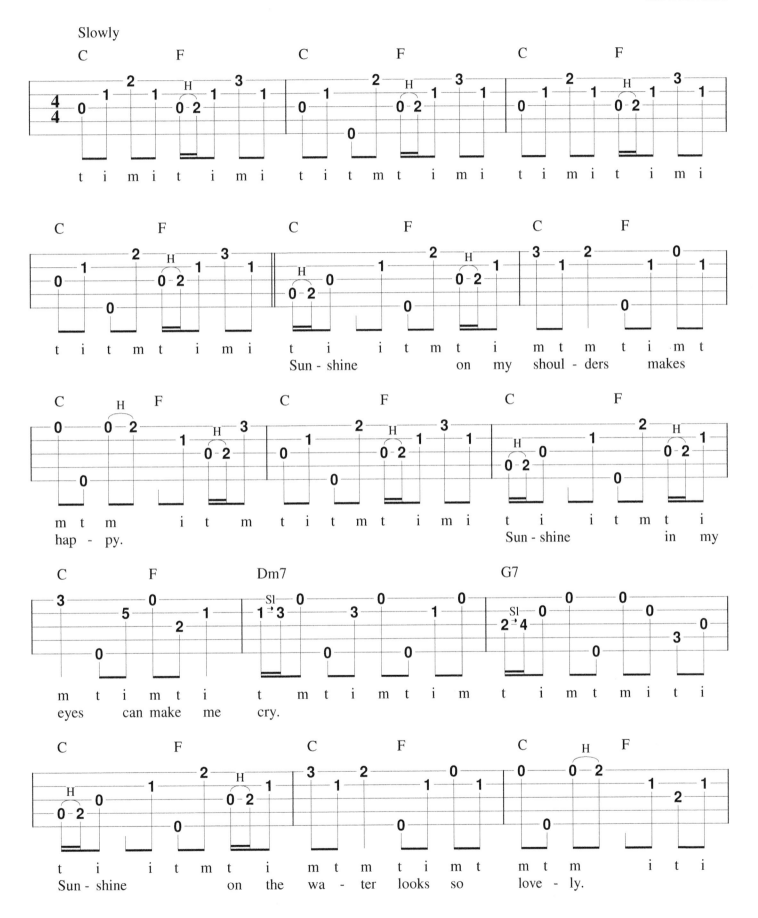

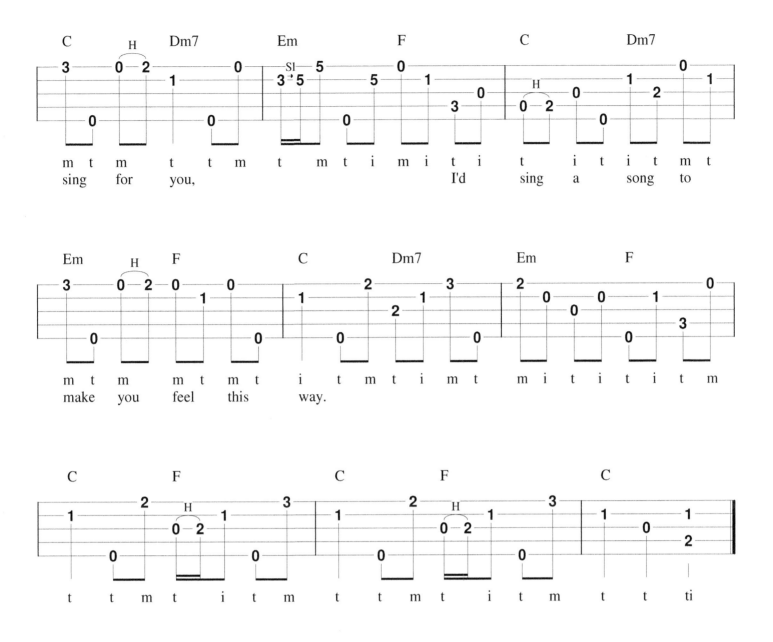

Refrain:
Sunshine on my shoulders makes me happy.
Sunshine in my eyes can make me cry.
Sunshine on the water looks so lovely.
Sunshine almost always makes me high.

2. If I had a tale that I could tell you,
   I'd tell a tale sure to make you smile.
   If I had a wish that I could wish for you,
   I'd make a wish for sunshine all the while.

Repeat Refrain

SWEET SURRENDER

from Walt Disney's THE BEARS AND I

Words and Music by
John Denver

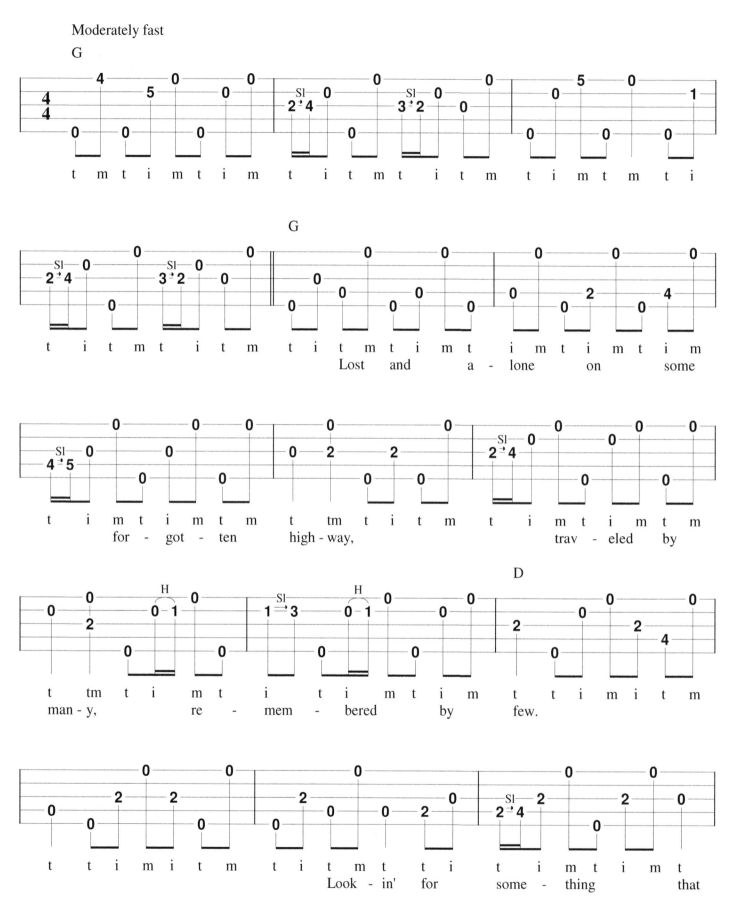

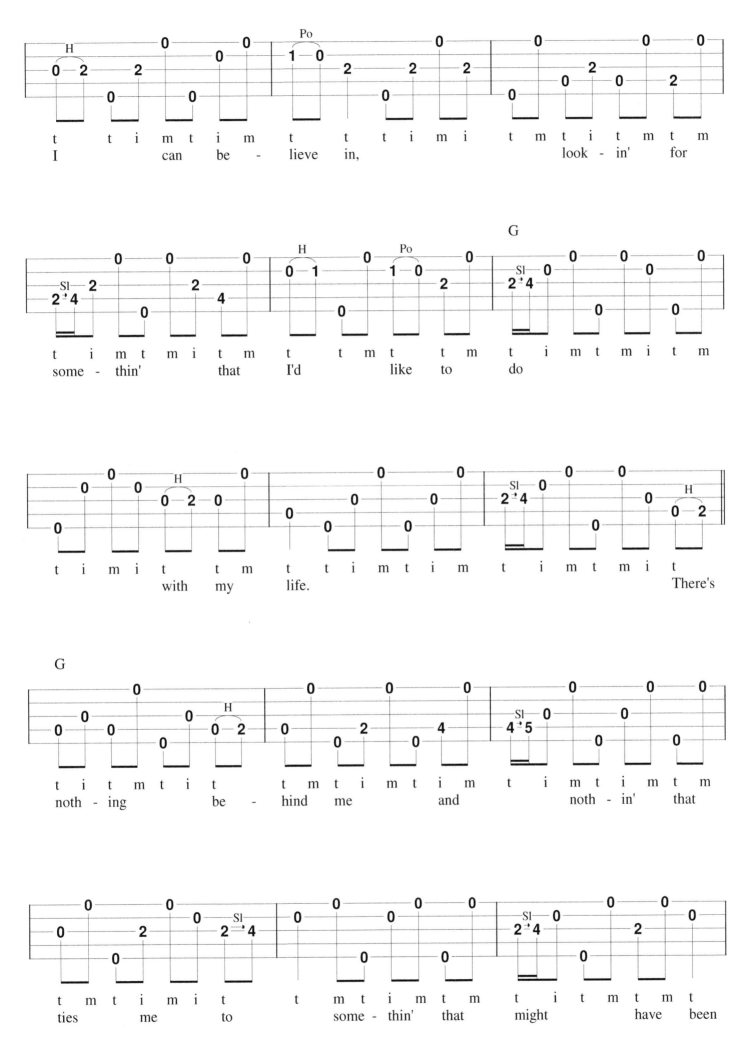

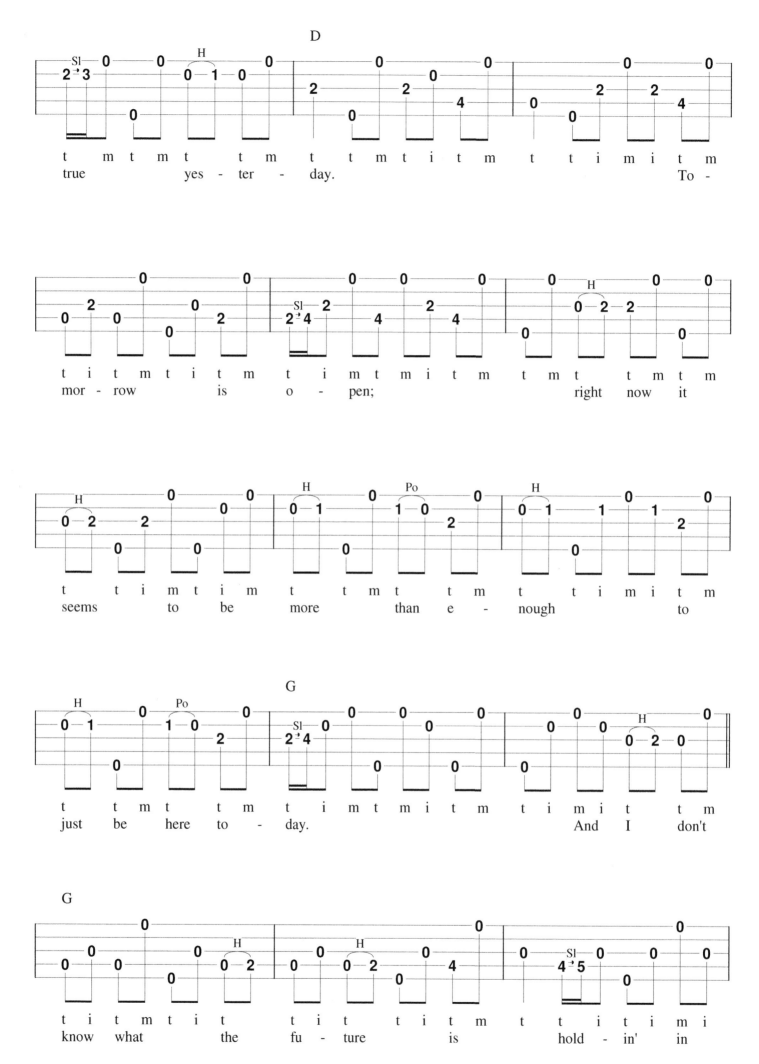

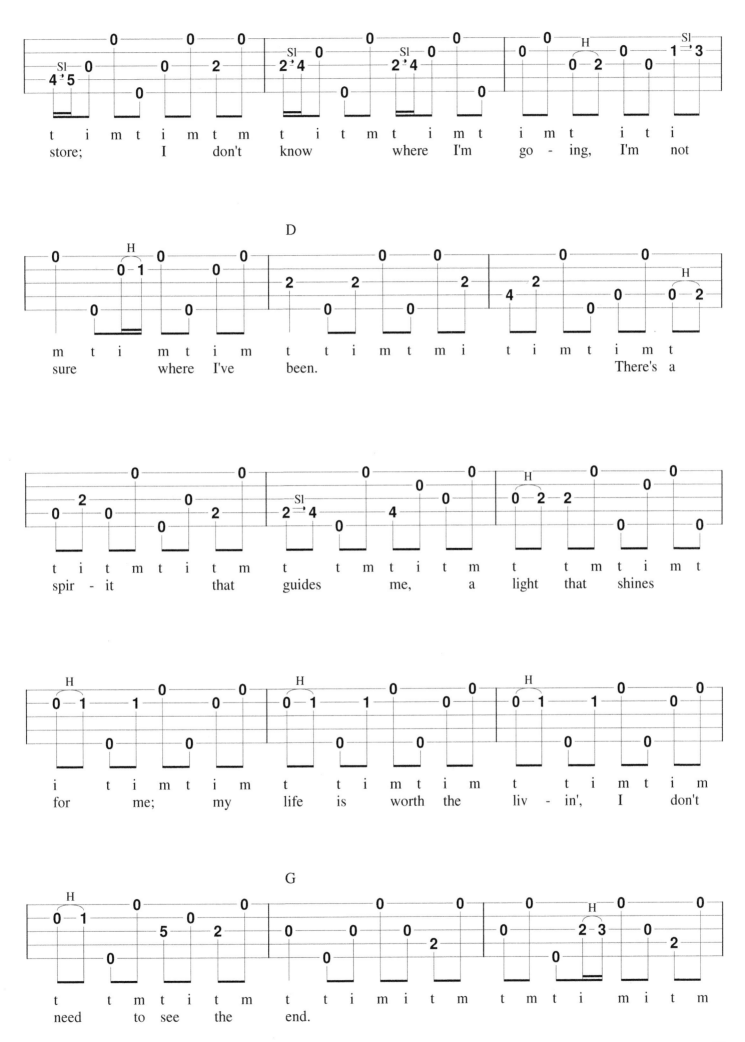

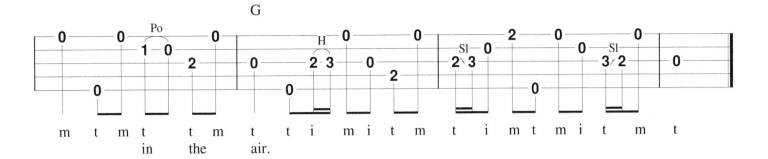

G

m   t   m t   t   m   t   t   i   m i   t   m   t   i   m t   m i   t   m   t

          in   the   air.

Chorus:
Sweet, sweet surrender, live, live without care.
Like a fish in the water, like a bird in the air.

4. Lost and alone on some forgotten highway,
   Traveled by many, remembered by few.
   Lookin' for something that I can believe in,
   Lookin' for something that I'd like to do with my life.

5. There's nothin' behind me and nothin' that ties me
   To somethin' that might have been true yesterday.
   Tomorrow is open; right now it seems to be more
   Than enough to just be here today.

6. And I don't know what the future is holdin' in store;
   I don't know where I'm goin', I'm not sure where I've been.
   There's a spirit that guides me, a light that shines for me;
   My life is worth the livin', I don't need to see the end.

   Repeat Chorus twice

TAKE ME HOME, COUNTRY ROADS

Words and Music by
John Denver, Bill Danoff
and Taffy Nivert

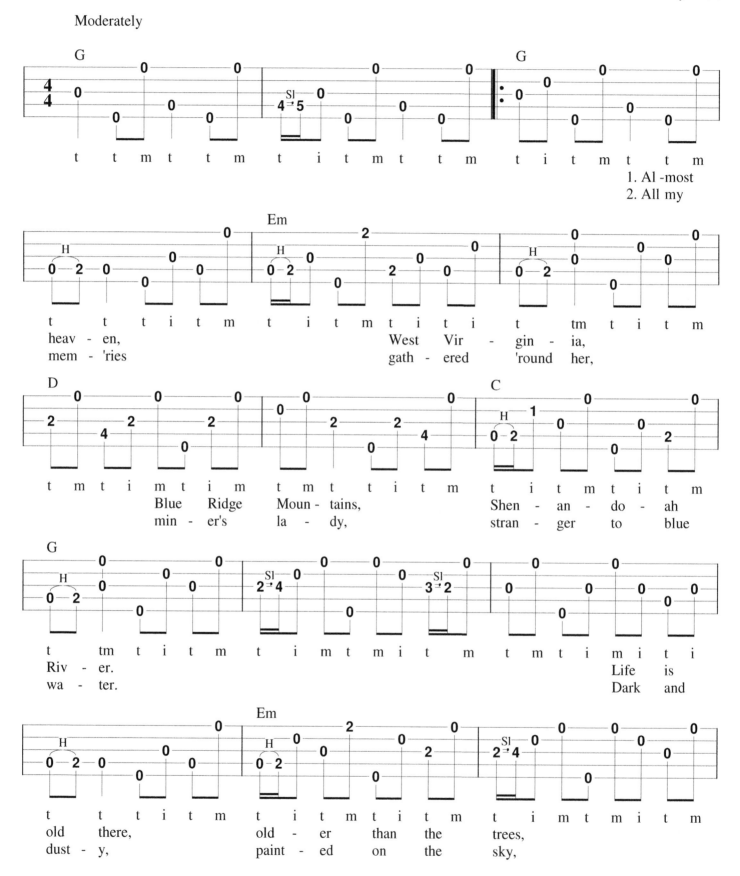

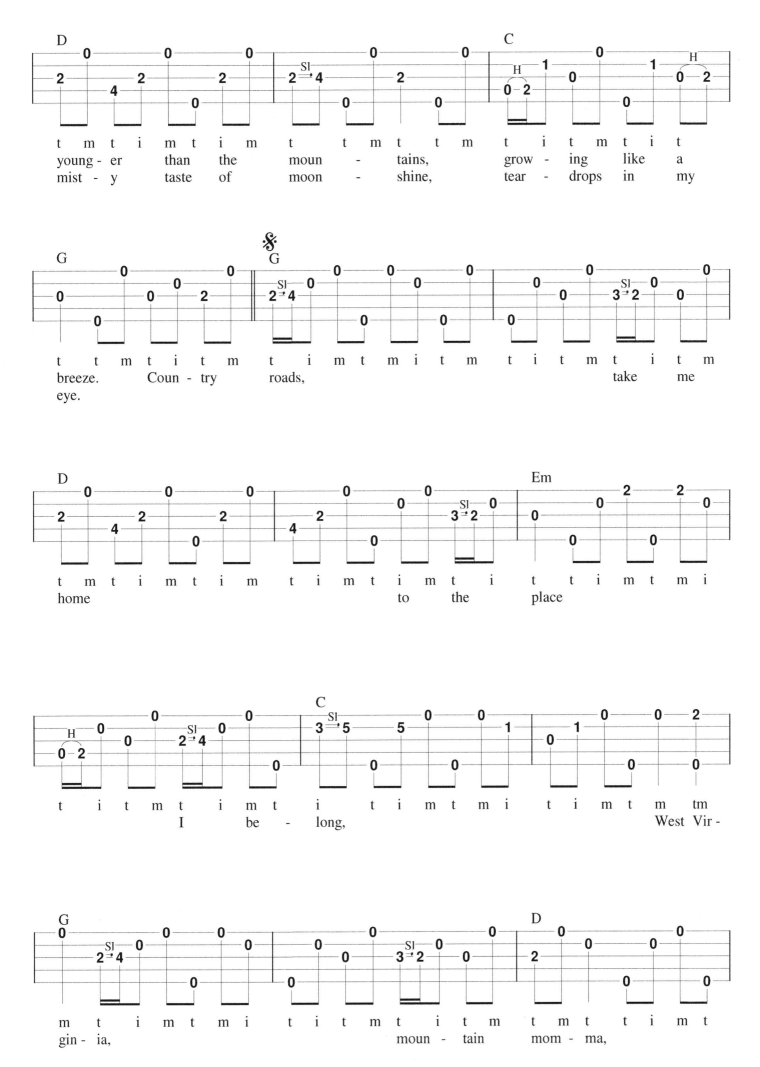

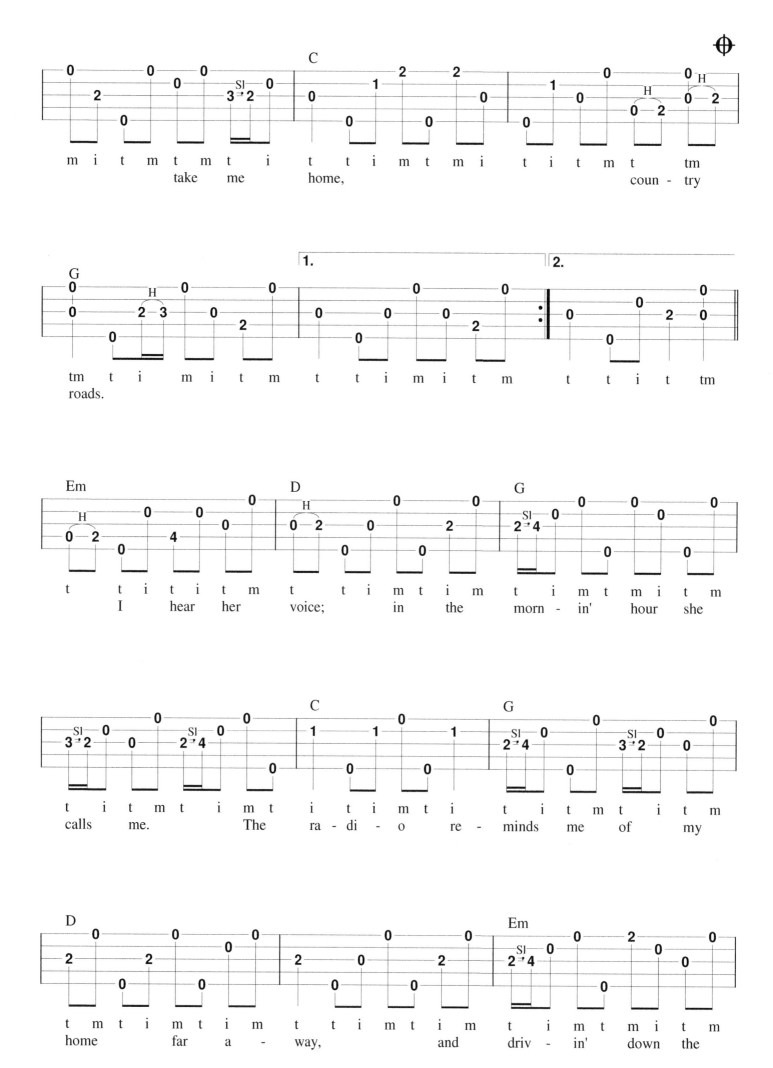

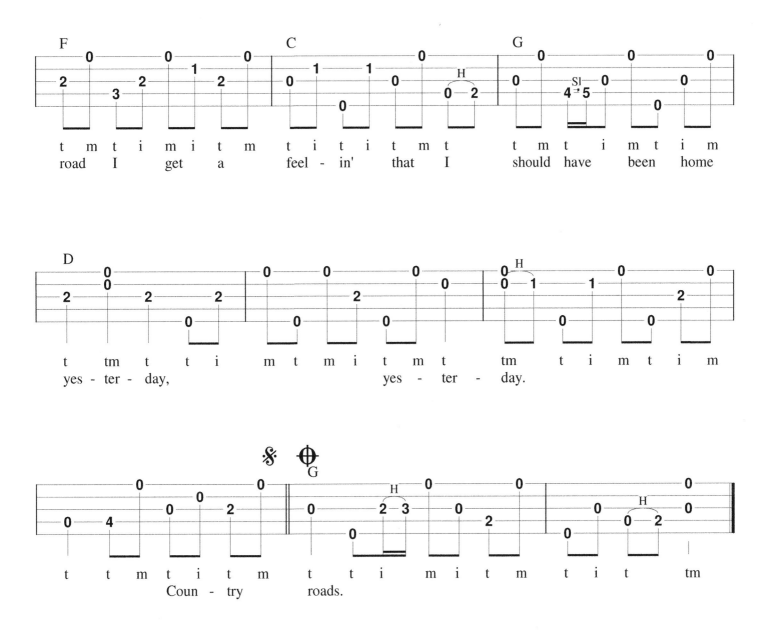

Chorus

Country Roads, take me home to the place I belong,
West Virginia, mountain momma, take me home, country roads.

Repeat Chorus

THANK GOD I'M A COUNTRY BOY

Words and Music by
John Martin Sommers

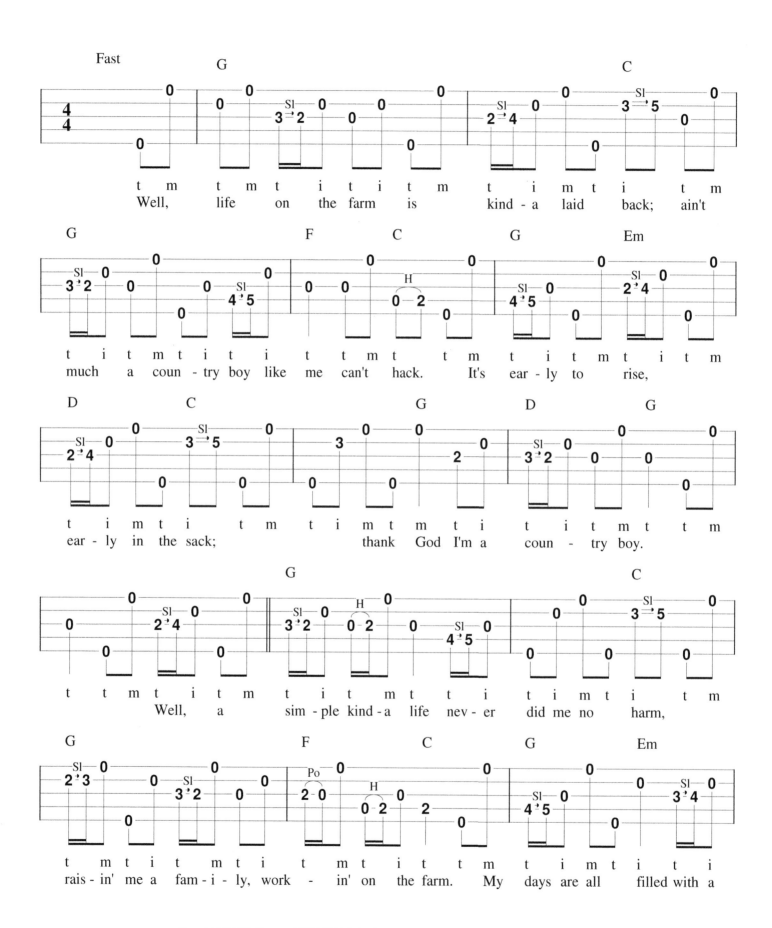

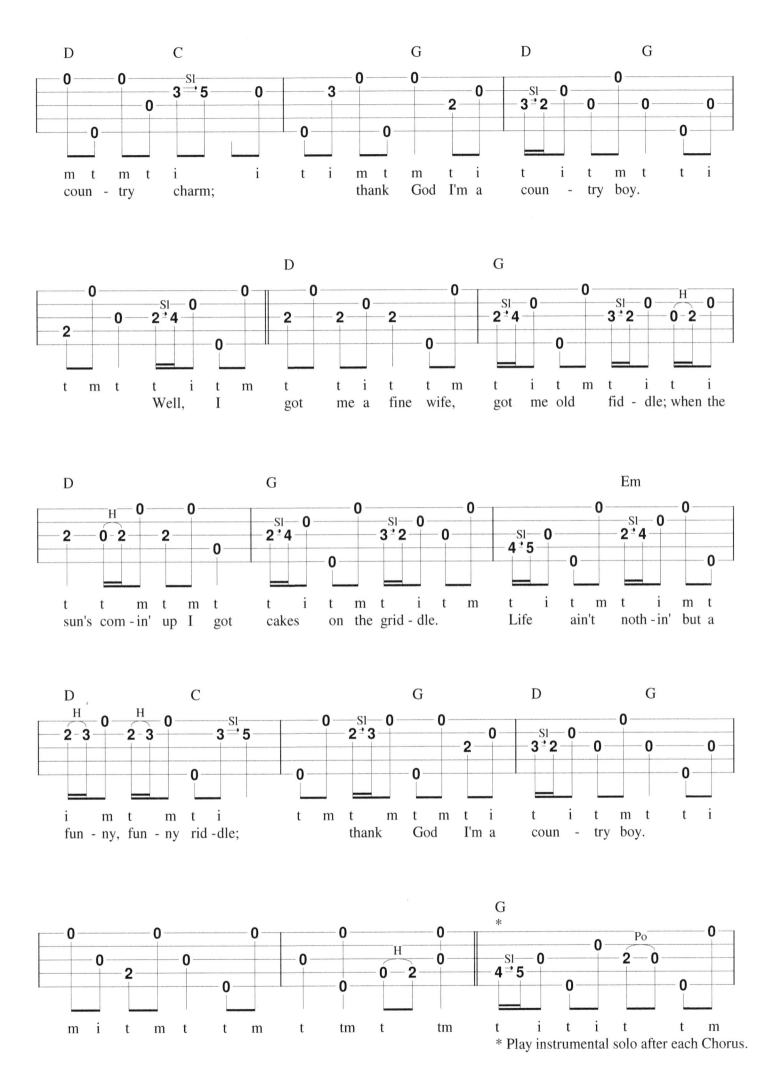

* Play instrumental solo after each Chorus.

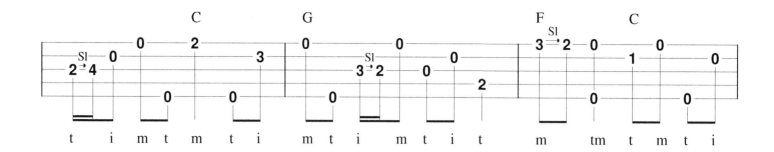

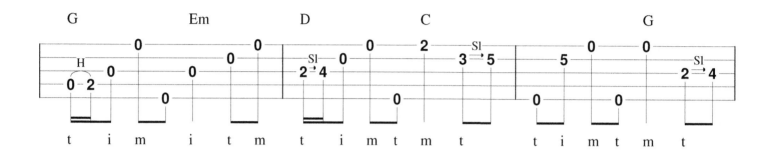

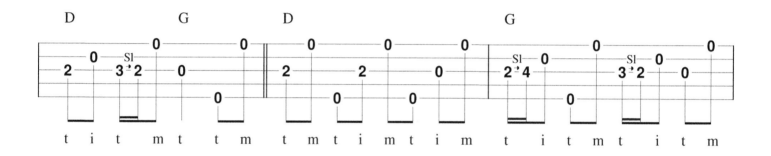

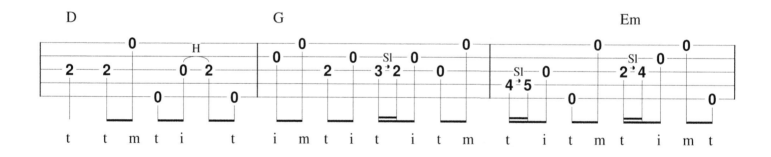

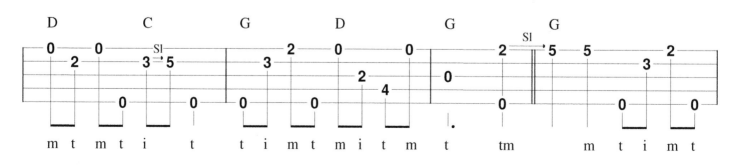

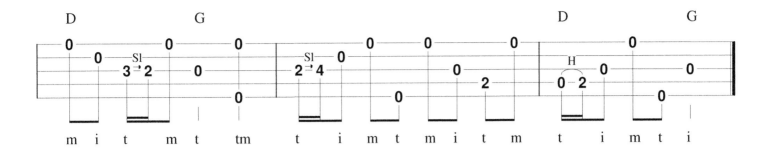

3. When the work's all done and the sun's settin' low,
   I pull out my fiddle and I rosin up the bow.
   The kids are asleep so I keep it kinda low; thank God I'm a country boy.

4. I'd play "Sally Goodin" all day if I could,
   But the Lord and my wife wouldn't take it very good.
   So I fiddle when I can, work when I should; thank God I'm a country boy.

   Chorus:
   Well, I got me a fine wife, I got me old fiddle;
   When the sun's comin' up I got cakes on the griddle.
   Life ain't nothin' but a funny, funny riddle; thank God I'm a country boy.

5. Well, I wouldn't trade my life for diamonds or jewels;
   I never was one of them money hungry fools.
   I'd rather have my fiddle and my farmin' tools; thank God I'm a country boy.

6. Well, city folk drivin' in a black limousine;
   A lotta sad people thinkin' that's a mighty keen.
   Son, let me tell ya now exactly what I mean; I thank God I'm a country boy.

   Repeat Chorus

7. Well, my fiddle was my daddy's till the day he died,
   And he took me by the hand and held me close to his side.
   He said; "Live a good life, play my fiddle with pride, and thank God you're a country boy."

8. My daddy taught me young how to hunt and how to whittle;
   He taught me how to work and play a tune on the fiddle.
   Taught me how to love and how to give just a little; thank God I'm a country boy.

   Repeat Chorus

THIS OLD GUITAR

Words and Music by
John Denver

Moderately

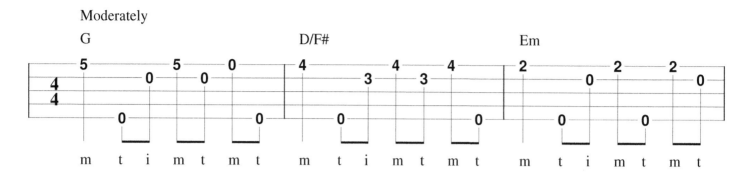

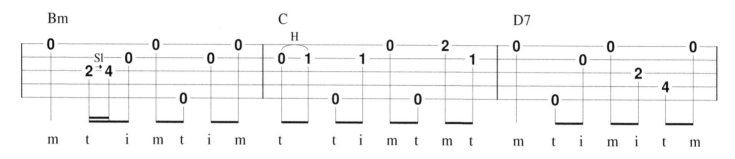

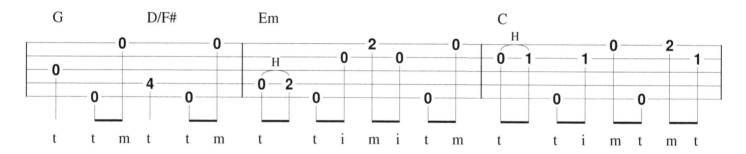

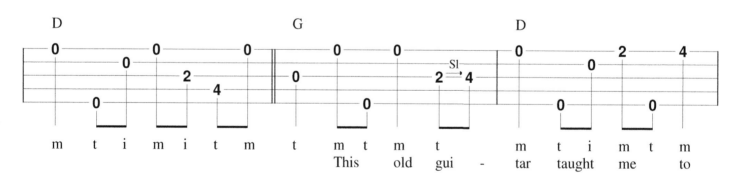

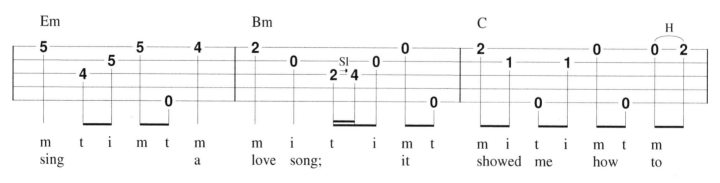

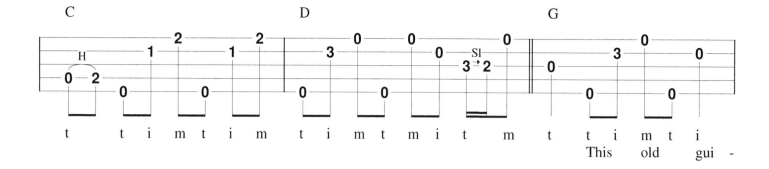

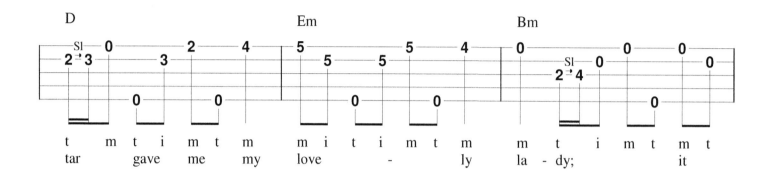

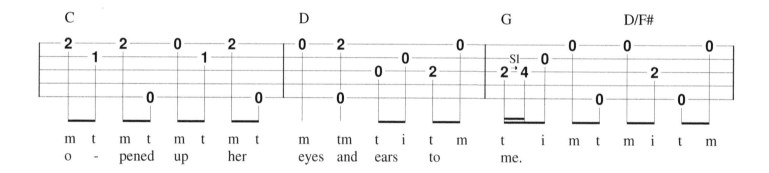

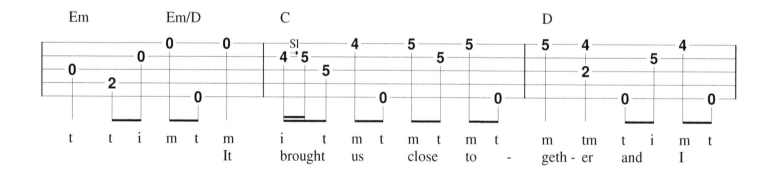

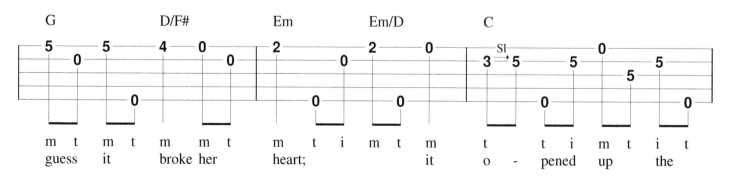

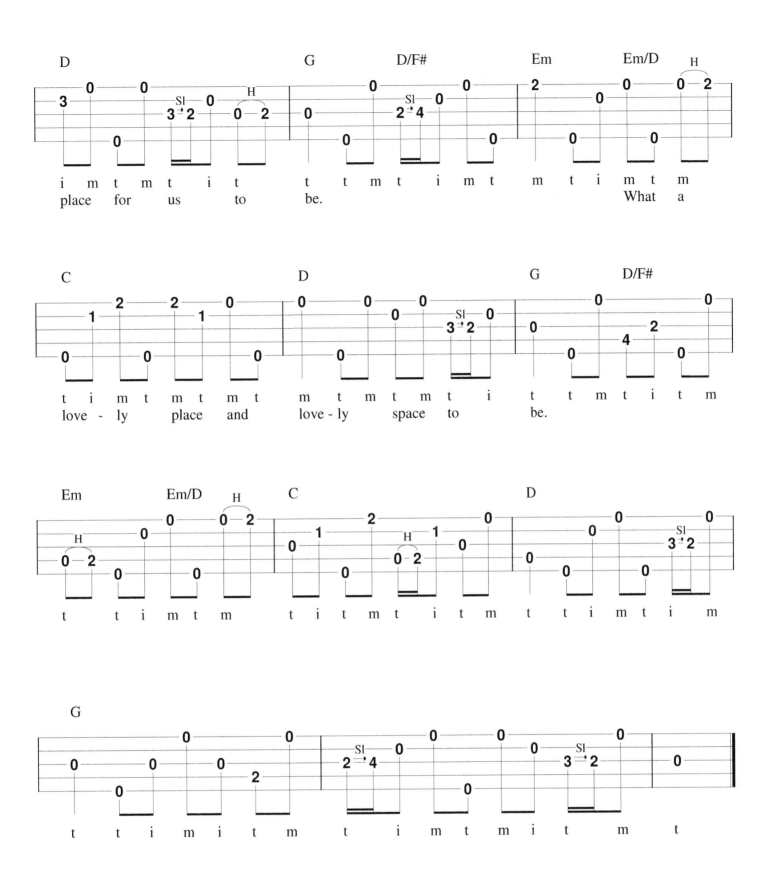

3. This old guitar gave me my life, my living,
   All the things you know I love to do.
   To serenade the stars that shine from a sunny mountainside,
   And most of all to sing my songs for you.
   I love to sing my songs for you, yes I do.
   You know, I love to sing my songs for you.

The Strum & Sing series for guitar and ukulele provides an unplugged and pared-down approach to your favorite songs – just the chords and the lyrics, with nothing fancy. These easy-to-play arrangements are designed for both aspiring and professional musicians.

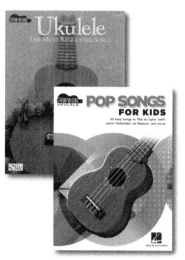

GUITAR

Acoustic Classics
00191891 ....$15.99

Adele
00159855 ....$12.99

Sara Bareilles
00102354 ....$12.99

The Beatles
00172234 ....$17.99

Blues
00159335 ....$12.99

Zac Brown Band
02501620 ....$19.99

Colbie Caillat
02501725 ....$14.99

Campfire Folk Songs
02500686 ....$15.99

Chart Hits of 2014-2015
00142554 ....$12.99

Chart Hits of 2015-2016
00156248 ....$12.99

Best of Kenny Chesney
00142457 ....$14.99

Christmas Carols
00348351 ....$14.99

Christmas Songs
00171332 ....$14.99

Kelly Clarkson
00146384 ....$14.99

Coffeehouse Songs for Guitar
00285991 ....$14.99

Leonard Cohen
00265489 ....$14.99

Dear Evan Hansen
00295108 ....$16.99

John Denver Collection
02500632 ....$17.99

Disney
00233900 ....$16.99

Eagles
00157994 ....$12.99

Easy Acoustic Songs
00125478 ....$19.99

Billie Eilish
00363094 ....$14.99

The Five-Chord Songbook
02501718 ....$12.99

Folk Rock Favorites
02501669 ....$14.99

Folk Songs
02501482 ....$14.99

The Four-Chord Country Songbook
00114936 ....$15.99

The Four Chord Songbook
02501533 ....$14.99

Four Chord Songs
00249581 ....$14.99

The Greatest Showman
00278383 ....$14.99

Hamilton
00217116 ....$15.99

Hymns
02501125 ....$8.99

Jack Johnson
02500858 ....$17.99

Robert Johnson
00191890 ....$12.99

Carole King
00115243 ....$10.99

Best of Gordon Lightfoot
00139393 ....$15.99

Dave Matthews Band
02501078 ....$10.95

John Mayer
02501636 ....$19.99

The Most Requested Songs
02501748 ....$14.99

Jason Mraz
02501452 ....$14.99

**Tom Petty –
Wildflowers & All the Rest**
00362682 ....$14.99

Elvis Presley
00198890 ....$12.99

Queen
00218578 ....$12.99

Rock Around the Clock
00103625 ....$12.99

Rock Ballads
02500872 ....$9.95

Rocketman
00300469 ....$17.99

Ed Sheeran
00152016 ....$14.99

The Six-Chord Songbook
02502277 ....$12.99

Chris Stapleton
00362625 ....$19.99

Cat Stevens
00116827 ....$17.99

Taylor Swift
00159856 ....$12.99

The Three-Chord Songbook
00211634 ....$12.99

Today's Hits
00119301 ....$12.99

Top Christian Hits
00156331 ....$12.99

Top Hits of 2016
00194288 ....$12.99

Keith Urban
00118558 ....$14.99

The Who
00103667 ....$12.99

Yesterday
00301629 ....$14.99

Neil Young – Greatest Hits
00138270 ....$15.99

UKULELE

The Beatles
00233899 ....$16.99

Colbie Caillat
02501731 ....$10.99

Coffeehouse Songs
00138238 ....$14.99

John Denver
02501694 ....$14.99

Folk Rock Favorites
00114600 ....$16.99

The 4-Chord Ukulele Songbook
00114331 ....$16.99

Jack Johnson
02501702 ....$19.99

John Mayer
02501706 ....$10.99

Ingrid Michaelson
02501741 ....$12.99

The Most Requested Songs
02501453 ....$14.99

Jason Mraz
02501753 ....$14.99

Pop Songs for Kids
00284415 ....$16.99

Sing-Along Songs
02501710 ....$15.99

HAL•LEONARD®
halleonard.com
Visit our website to see full song lists
or order from your favorite retailer.

*Prices, contents and availability
subject to change without notice.*

More Great Piano/Vocal Books

FROM CHERRY LANE

For a complete listing of Cherry Lane titles available,
including contents listings, please visit our web site at

www.cherrylane.com

Cherry Lane Music is your source for
JOHN DENVER SONGBOOKS!

PIANO/VOCAL BOOKS

JOHN DENVER ANTHOLOGY
A collection of 54 of this music legend's greatest tunes, including: Annie's Song • Follow Me • Leaving on a Jet Plane • Rocky Mountain High • Sunshine on My Shoulders • and more, plus a biography and John's reflections on his many memorable songs.
02502165 Piano/Vocal/Guitar $22.95

JOHN DENVER ANTHOLOGY
Easy arrangements of 34 of the finest from this beloved artist. Includes: Follow Me • Grandma's Feather Bed • Leaving on a Jet Plane • Matthew • Perhaps Love • Rocky Mountain High • Sunshine on My Shoulders • Thank God I'm a Country Boy • and many more.
02501366 Easy Piano $19.99

THE BEST OF JOHN DENVER – EASY PIANO
A collection of 18 Denver classics arranged for easy piano. Contains: Leaving on a Jet Plane • Take Me Home, Country Roads • Rocky Mountain High • Follow Me • and more.
02505512 Easy Piano.. $9.95

THE BEST OF JOHN DENVER – PIANO SOLOS
Best of John Denver – Piano Solos is a fabulous collection of 10 greatest hits from the legendary country artist. It includes many of his major hits including: Annie's Song • Leaving on a Jet Plane • Rocky Mountain High • and Take Me Home, Country Roads.
02503629 Piano Solo $10.95

A JOHN DENVER CHRISTMAS
A delightful collection of Christmas songs and carols recorded by John Denver. Includes traditional carols (Deck the Halls • Hark! The Herald Angels Sing • The Twelve Days of Christmas) as well as such contemporary songs as: A Baby Just Like You • Christmas for Cowboys • Christmas Like a Lullaby • and The Peace Carol.
02500002 Piano/Vocal/Guitar $14.95

JOHN DENVER: THE COMPLETE LYRICS
An extremely gifted singer/songwriter, John Denver possessed the unique ability to marry melodic music with gentle, thought-provoking words that endeared him to his countless fans. Now, for the first time ever, John Denver's lyrics have been printed in their entirety: no other book like this exists! It contains lyrics to more than 200 songs, and includes an annotated discography showing all the songs, and an index of first lines. This collection also features an introduction by Tom Paxton, and a foreword from Milt Okun, John Denver's first record producer, and the founder of Cherry Lane Music.
02500459 .... $16.95

JOHN DENVER'S GREATEST HITS
This collection combines all of the songs from Denver's three best-selling greatest hits albums. 34 songs in all, including: Leaving on a Jet Plane • For Baby (For Bobbie) • Thank God I'm a Country Boy • Annie's Song • Perhaps Love • I Want to Live.
02502166 Piano/Vocal/Guitar $17.95

JOHN DENVER – A LEGACY OF SONG
This collection celebrates one of the world's most popular and prolific entertainers. Features 25 of John's best-loved songs with his commentary on each: Annie's Song • Fly Away • Leaving on a Jet Plane • Rocky Mountain High • Sunshine on My Shoulders • Take Me Home, Country Roads • Thank God I'm a Country Boy • and more, plus a biography, discography, reflections on John's numerous accomplishments, and photos spanning his entire career.
02502151 Piano/Vocal/Guitar Softcover................................ $24.95

JOHN DENVER & THE MUPPETS – A CHRISTMAS TOGETHER
Back by popular demand! This book featuring John Denver, Kermit, and all the Muppets includes 12 holiday songs: A Baby Just like You • Carol for a Christmas Tree • Christmas Is Coming • The Christmas Wish • Deck the Halls • Have Yourself a Merry Little Christmas • Little Saint Nick • Noel: Christmas Eve, 1913 • The Peace Carol • Silent Night, Holy Night • The Twelve Days of Christmas • We Wish You a Merry Christmas.
02500501 Piano/Vocal/Guitar $9.95

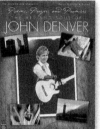

POEMS, PRAYERS AND PROMISES: THE ART AND SOUL OF JOHN DENVER
Book/CD Pack
This songbook/CD pack is a must for John Denver fans, who will not want to miss the large color section featuring his never-before-published nature and travel photography, concert memorabilia and new interviews about his songwriting craft with the people who knew and worked with him. The 23 Denver classics include: Annie's Song • Leaving on a Jet Plane • Sunshine on My Shoulders • and more.
02500566 Piano/Vocal/Guitar $19.95

JOHN DENVER – THE WILDLIFE CONCERT
This matching folio to John Denver's second live album – a two-CD set accompanying a cable TV special and home video – features 29 fabulous tracks: Amazon • Annie's Song • Bet on the Blues • Calypso • Darcy Farrow • Eagles and Horses • Falling Out of Love • The Harder They Fall • Is It Love? • Leaving on a Jet Plane • Me and My Uncle • A Song for All Lovers • Sunshine on My Shoulders • You Say That the Battle Is Over • and more.
_____ 02500326 Piano/Vocal/Guitar............................. $17.95

P/V/G SHEET MUSIC

02504223	**Annie's Song**..................................	$3.95
02504181	**For You**..	$3.99
02504225	**Leaving on a Jet Plane**	$3.95
02509538	**Perhaps Love**..................................	$3.95
02504219	**Sunshine on My Shoulders**	$3.95
02504214	**Take Me Home, Country Roads**	$3.95

GUITAR BOOKS

JOHN DENVER ANTHOLOGY FOR EASY GUITAR
This superb collection of 42 great Denver songs made easy for guitar includes: Annie's Song • Leaving on a Jet Plane • Take Me Home, Country Roads • plus performance notes, a biography, and Denver's thoughts on the songs.
02506878 Easy Guitar $15.95

JOHN DENVER AUTHENTIC GUITAR STYLE
12 never-before-published acoustic guitar note-for-note transcriptions of the most popular songs by John Denver. Includes the hits: Annie's Song • Sunshine on My Shoulders • Take Me Home, Country Roads • and more.
02506901 Acoustic Guitar Transcriptions $14.95

THE BEST OF JOHN DENVER
Over 20 of Denver's best-known hits spanning his 25-year career! Includes: Annie's Song • Leaving on a Jet Plane • Rocky Mountain High • Thank God I'm a Country Boy • Sunshine on My Shoulders • and more.
02506879 Easy Guitar $9.95

JOHN DENVER COLLECTION
Strum & Sing Series
A great unplugged and pared-down collection of chords and lyrics for 40 favorite John Denver songs, including: Annie's Song • Calypso • Fly Away • Follow Me • Higher Ground • Rocky Mountain High • Take Me Home, Country Roads • This Old Guitar • and more.
02500632 Guitar/Vocal $9.95

JOHN DENVER – FOLK SINGER
15 songs transcribed note for note from this country-folk entertainer and humanitarian. Includes: Fly Away • I Guess He'd Rather Be in Colorado • Mother Nature's Son • Potter's Wheel • Take Me Home, Country Roads • Thirsty Boots • This Old Guitar • Today • and more.
02500984 Play-It-Like-It-Is Guitar......................................$19.95

JOHN DENVER – GREATEST HITS FOR FINGERSTYLE GUITAR
For the first time ever, 11 favorite Denver standards in fingerstyle arrangements that incorporate the melodies of the songs and can therefore be played as solo guitar pieces or vocal accompaniments. Includes: Annie's Song • Leaving on a Jet Plane • Rocky Mountain High • and more.
02506928 Fingerstyle Guitar $14.95